1 SUSPENSION

ACKNOWLEDGEMENTS

The author's considerable gratitude goes to those who have helped to make this book possible, as well as contributing substantially to his patchy technical education in their various ways.

Special thanks to :

John Beattie
Richard Blackmore
Frank Bott
Jim Boursos
John Bright
Tony Cotton
Ryan Currier
Frank Dernie
Graham Easter
Tony Gilhome
David Gould
Keith Gowers
Richard Hurdwell
National Motor Museum, Beaulieu
Steve Owen
Brian Redman
Jeremy Rossitter
Ray Rowan
Fred Smith
Darell Staniforth
Clive Spackman
Joe Ward
Reverend Barry Whitehead
Frank Williams

and paticularly :

Trevor Harris
Gordon Murray
Tony Southgate
Peter Wright

COMPETITION CAR
SUSPENSION
DESIGN·CONSTRUCTION·TUNING

ALLAN STANIFORTH

A **FOULIS** Motoring Book

First published 1988

© RACECAR ENGINEERING & Allan Staniforth

Published by:
Haynes Publishing Group, Sparkford, Near Yeovil,
Somerset BA22 7JJ, England.

Haynes Publications Inc.
861 Lawrence Drive, Newbury Park, California, 91320,
USA.

Produced for G.T. Foulis & Co. Ltd. by
RACECAR ENGINEERING (Specialist Publications)
6, Foundry House, Stars Lane, Yeovil, Somerset BA20
1NL, England.

Editorial Director: Ian Bamsey
Research Assistant: Alan Lis

Drawings by: Darell Staniforth & Alan Lis

British Library Cataloguing in Publication Data

Staniforth, Allan
Race car technology.
1. Racing cars. Suspension. Design
I. Title
629.2'43

ISBN 0-85429-645-X

Library of Congress Catalog Card number 88-80559

Printed in England by:
Wincanton Litho, Wincanton, Somerset
DTP & Artwork by:
Graphic Examples, Sherborne, Dorset

CONTENTS

The Reasons Why

...an introduction

1

The wheel and the axle are not quite as old as the average hill but they still go back a bit. The path from a slice of tree trunk to an F1 rear is a long one, well worthy of a story all to itself, but we shall be more concerned here with all the complexities of holding it on the vehicle, controlling how it does its job and utilising the small area where it touches the road to the very ultimate. In a word: suspension.

In the early stages of the evolutionary path suspension did not, of course, exist. It was sufficient that man had devised a means to transport, however laboriously, objects that had hitherto been immovable. But war and sport (the latter often a thinly disguised derivative of the former) were incentives to rapid progress. The Romans were a shining example. The Legions had carts and the Colosseum had chariot racing, without doubt the Formula One of the day. Neither appear to have used suspension but the strong metal-tyred spoked wheel had already appeared in the form it would still be taking 2000 years later on the horse drawn English brewery drays of the 20th century.

Why bother to explain or illustrate the past at all? Because nothing happens in a vacuum. Everybody except the first to do something (often much further back than one might suspect) is copying to some degree, even if unknowingly. History has an extraordinary number of instances of major inventions made by different people in different parts of the world at about the same time, within milli-seconds of each other if you think in cosmic terms, that is in millions of years. Bitter are the disputes and accusations within science and industry when this happens.

So it is that a glance back (in no way totally comprehensive) will hopefully show how history and the designers it left behind laid the groundwork. What died and what survived is a fascinating insight into the state of the art not readily obtainable in any other way.

Despite computers and huge budgets, it is still an art at the highest level. While cars undoubtedly now tend to work very much better 'straight out of the box' the legendary performer is still nurtured by secret and ferociously intense testing and changes between that well known box and the first grid. Assuming the engine is good and the chassis is as rigid as possible (quite separate problems) how the car handles, its ability to put its power down and behave in the way a world class driver asks of it is almost totally down to

Classic suspension on a classic car. These shots of the 1970 Ferrari 512 5.0 litre, 12 cylinder Sports-Prototype illustrate the traditional mid-engined car layout with inclined coil spring/ damper unit operated directly by the upright at the rear and by its support on lower wishbone at the front.

suspension.

Some would say "or lack of it" as one design parameter is often to reduce movement to almost nil on the premise that if a problem is currently insoluble you eliminate what is causing it. Construing this as a bit defeatist, later chapters will be aimed at getting the best of both worlds. This is not to ignore aerodynamics but downforce still has to be reacted through the suspension.

With the fundamentals fairly firmly established, success can often stem from brilliant detail, ingenious installation or integration and simplicity. Better materials, refinements in small or sophisticated ways often give immeasurably better results than attempts to re-invent the wheel.

At the top of the motor racing tree, as in virtually all highly technological fields, money is effectively unlimited with the most highly skilled of craftsmen, most ingenious and talented designers all working for the best dozen or so drivers in the world, welded together by the most able team leaders. It can be such a formidable combination that even in the top echelons there can still be second and third raters, relatively speaking. Characteristics include coming into the pits on the first lap, having gear knobs fall off, failing to tighten plugs or wheel nuts, blowing engines and fitting incorrect gears. Such things rarely happen more than once to the top operators.

In many ways engine power was the name of the game for years. Suspension with all its intricacies, unknowns and hopelessly interrelated variables was a bit of a slow starter, making little impression in Britain until the Sixties, in America until the Seventies (and, some wit might aver, at Ferrari until the Eighties). Taking our trip back into history, we find even well before the arrival of the internal combustion engine suspension of major concern to certain vehicle builders. As still today away from the race track, the reason was comfort.

The leaf spring in a variety of forms from quarter to double elliptic, with the necessary pivoting shackles and location on the chassis and axle was of vital concern to the well-named 'carriage trade'. The wealthy have always, by and large, demanded the best, so far as they could distinguish it. Whether technically minded or not, the long distance traveller's backside told him more than his brain about the quality of his purchase.

The farm cart, trans-Prairie Conestoga wagons and early stage coaches all relied upon the solidly mounted axle. The

Brougham, later stages and the Hansom cab were the leaders in the new generation of comfortable transport. Both the theory and the practice of the Ackerman angle approach to steering front wheels with reduced or minimum scrub were known before the first Benz stuttered into life.

It was sensible and obvious that the first engines were hung into or on horse drawn carriages, needing only a bicycle-style chain drive to an existing axle. It took the pioneers no time flat to realise that a suspended axle, moving with road shock needed to move about known arcs or lines if the chain was not to break.

Probably the best of several solutions was to insert a chassis mounted cross-shaft to which engine power went first. This was located on the same line as the forward pick-ups of the rear leaf spring. A secondary chain then ran from the cross-shaft to the rear axle. When the axle rose or fell, both it and the chain moved about a common axis and thus followed the same path.

The front already had suspension and moveable wheels linked to horse shafts. Reversing the linkage after the departure of the horse, and bringing it off one side rather than centrally gave the fundamentals of a remotely steered suspension that would survive for some considerable time. And these first cars were the racers of the day, from the moment contemporary sportsmen (and a few rare ladies) perceived that they had a brand new instrument with which to compete against their fellows.

Goggles, cloth caps and helmets did not in those early days immediately indicate a racing driver. They were essential protection for any motorist sitting out in the open at the mercy of wind and rain. Racing cars emerged as a separate breed quite slowly, with emphasis on engine development and light weight. In many ways road and race car development ran parallel, cross-pollination at first improving the racers, then the racers improving the road versions.

A front beam axle with a leaf spring each side proved admirably suited to accepting the move of the newer multi-cylindered engines to the front, this in its turn requiring a clutch and gearbox feeding rearwards into a shaft.

Industry had driven a gear on a shaft by means of a pinion gear at right angles to it for more than two centuries. It offered a method of driving the rear wheels in enclosed oilbath conditions that was to totally oust the chain. (Not without a rearguard action by the famed Frazer Nash sports cars which were still being propelled via chain in the early

Thirties).

The new geared rear axle could also be both located and sprung very conveniently on a pair of parallel leaf springs. Pre World War One, this layout was becoming common both on road and track with little or no alteration for the latter, and there is a strong case that the passenger car industry, particularly in America pioneered many of the steps over the next 40 years. Independent front suspension, coil springs, the MacPherson strut, rear axles with varying degrees of sophistication in location, plus wider, fatter tyres for good measure were all road car developments. Virtually everything had one target - the soft ride.

What gave Britain and Europe such a golden opportunity - or urgent need - for improved roadholding was, as has been frequently pointed out, a road system of twists and turns and uphill and downhill rather than flat and straight lined. It spawned a tradition of sports cars in Aston Martin, Alfa Romeo, Bentley, Delage, Hispano Suiza, Bugatti, MG and a dozen others between the wars (not to mention the occasional sporting car from a mass manufacturer, notably Austin).

The inter-war sports car manufacturers shared two things - a constant struggle to get more engine power and reliability and a tendency to remain faithful to the beam axle with leaf springs. Improvements in handling came partly from a lighter body with a lower vehicle centre of gravity, and partly from much stiffer springing (leaf springs tightly bound with cord to increase the rate were a fairly common sight) limiting roll and unwanted wheel movements.

The precision of the handling and acceleration if not the comfort improved dramatically with this treatment over the saloons from which many sports cars drew their basic parts. A perfect example was the contrast between the dreadful roll-oversteering, gutless and almost brakeless early Austin Seven and the Nippy or more exotic Ulster from the same factory. Basically the same, they were a transformation in driving quality.

Only after a second World War followed by space research released a torrent of technology did the face of motor racing begin to change massively and rapidly. Commercial backing, the cash with advertising so contemptuously spurned in earlier years, did the rest.

What are now known as Sports-Prototypes (or Stateside, as Prototypes) were quick off the mark with the factory developed derivatives of the great sports cars of the period. From

Napier, Delage and Renault to Alfa Romeo, Bugatti and Aston Martin, racing had previously been largely a two man affair. Friction dampers remotely controlled by a riding mechanic, together with manually operated lubrication for the suspension - perhaps the true forerunners of late Eighties active suspension technician with pits to car radio link and data logging to help modify computerised suspension settings!

The Sports-Prototype started life as a genuine sports car which, even in the early Fifties, an amateur could buy off the shelf and race competitively. However, at that time it quickly became apparent that cars which handled superbly at high road speeds showed painful shortcomings when really pushed to the limit. They rolled to extreme degrees, assumed odd wheel angles, tore tyres to pieces variously front or rear, outer edge or inner, had wheel twirling steering and what came to be known in every paddock bar as understeer, or oversteer, or both.

The amateurs - read anyone who did not own a factory - set about their own modifications as best they might. The factories - Jaguar for one with the C and D-Types - generally kept the engine and the bonnet badge while building another, vastly better handling car to carry the marque to victory. Spectators saw the familiar badge on a sometimes familiar, sometimes dramatically new body. Mostly they did not see redesigned "production" suspension, different springs, new patterns of damper, the early experiments with independent rear suspension, racing tyres, reduced weight and sometimes double the production power.

Formula One had already embarked upon its single minded approach to being the fastest thing on four wheels around a road circuit. But it had tended to always emphasise the engine and had been an affair of either countries (Germany with Mercedes and Auto Union - massive finance and power and horrific handling) or the rich talented customers of bespoke builders like ERA, Ferrari, the Maserati brothers producing essentially light, narrow single seater versions of sports cars, still with a preponderance of beam and solid axles and leaf springs, though with much experiment and refinement in location.

The true revolution in suspension design began in both camps - when John Cooper put the engine in the back and combined it with transverse leaf springs, wishbones and anti-roll bars but questionable geometry, and Colin Chapman put coil springs and sophisticated wishbone

Inter war cars such as the 1930 Alfa Romeo (previous page) and the 1931 Aston Martin (right) sports machines clung to the beam axle. Note that both have leaf spring suspended solid rear axles - effectively a beam - as at the front.

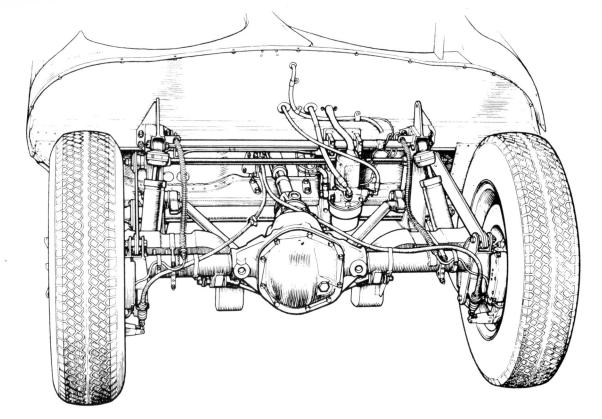

control of wheel angles under the skin of his early sports/racers (though they stayed front-engined for a curiously long time considering the magnitude of his thinking).

Chapman spelled out for the observant the needs and aims of racing suspension that have held valid for a quarter of a century, being copied or adapted, modified or developed wherever cars race. They are covered later in greater detail but in broad terms might be defined as keeping the wheel and tyre vertical to the road surface at all times, eliminating alterations caused by squat or nose-dive, road bumps or roll in corners and keeping the roll centre in one place and track constant.

Up to now perfection in all of these has proved impossible, but in the course of seeking it, all four wheels are independently sprung and connected through massive hubs to rigid links in pure tension and compression, which in their turn are attached to the vehicle via metal/metal spherical joints at rigid points in its structure.

None of these parts should be an ounce heavier than is necessary to deal with the forces involved, and when under load on the move should not allow the wheels/tyres to adopt unwanted toe-in or out or any other unplanned movements.

By the time of the mid engine era Sports-Prototypes were enclosed wheel, long distance versions of the Formula One

The Fifties D-Type Jaguar was a purposed-designed Le Mans racer with a monocoque centre section, and the rear suspension was hung from the back bulkhead as shown here.
The axle was a production item located by (non standard) pairs of trailing arms and the springing medium was a single (centrally located) torsion bar which linked between trailing arm pivots.

sprinters and by the Eighties they had all finally arrived at five extraordinary similarities. Whatever else they did not share, almost every successful Sports-Prototype and Grand Prix car shared: i) unequal length wishbones to locate the wheel/hub unit; ii) a coil spring to permit some degree of bump and rebound for the wheel; iii) an oil or oil/air filled valved damper to control the spring's inclination to go ge-doing, ge-doing, ge-doing unless restrained; iv) usually, though not always an anti roll bar of varying degrees of sophistication to reduce and control lean; v) effectively invisible, the geometry of the links, and the effect they have on the wheels as they swing through their various arcs.

The suspension systems of successful cars varied in detail, materials and complication but not in principle. Even the advanced and esoteric world of Active suspension was, at the time of writing, in essence, exactly what has just been described. The only difference was that the coil and damper had been combined and given a new lease of life through a remote and virtually instantaneously adjustable hydraulic system. The mystery was, given the same basic layout, why did not all conventional systems work with the same degree of success? There is, at least for the time being, no answer to that. The number of variables is so great, with every altera-tion causing something else to alter, and so on and so on down the line, that as yet there are not enough hours in a racing day, week or season, even with computer assistance, to get it all together to a state of perfection. And even that statement assumes some definition of 'perfection', which happens to be lacking.

In the real world, designers and constructors are continu-ally forced to strike a balance between conflicting targets. One man's idea of "optimum" will rarely be that of another. Needless to say, some clearly get it more right than others, while the line between success and failure grows ever more fine. But the lure and challenge of being the best in the world, particularly at a Grand Epreuve or Le Mans, or Indianapolis are more than enough to ensure a long line of hopeful aspirants. Ahead of the reader lie no magic solu-tions, only a path of sorts through the jungle. To the would-be designer, a student of the art, the knowledgeable pad-dock prowler, or anyone else fascinated by the deceptive simplicity of Grand Prix, Le Mans and Indy cars all that follows is dedicated.

Suspension does not work in isolation any more than any other part of a racing vehicle. It cannot be mounted where

The most powerful road racing car of the pre-ground effect era was the 5.4 litre turbocharged Porsche 917/30 Can Am car of 1973: it was rated 1,100 b.h.p. It had a spaceframe chassis but its suspension (right) is broadly similar to that of the rival monocoque Chevrolet-McLaren M20 (left).

the driver will sit or the crankshaft will revolve. Pull rods might be impossible to employ due to a lack of a point of sufficient strength on which to mount the necessary rockers. Space will always be at a premium, and available materials may limit what can be done though this will hardly affect those at the top of the tree. They operate in a world of effectively unlimited money just so long as they can balance on the edge of the financial precipice. Fall over the edge and they are back to mild steel, a fibreglass kit and second-hand rubber.

Strength and reliability with minimum weight are vital. Protection from heat may prove essential. Complicated linkage with inevitable risk of failure may be forced upon a designer. Some degree of alteration may save a team in mid season. Accessibility with its partner, speed of replacement, may save a team in mid race (at least in endurance events).

Though now growing rare, a radical technical change such as from cross-ply to radial tyre could demand not only totally new suspension geometry, rather than simple adjustments to increase static negative camber for radials, but a new chassis to accept that suspension.

Aerodynamics can double or triple the weight of the car at high speeds, and consequently the physical loads being fed into many components.

But all of these are still only peripheral complications to what is the heart of the matter: getting the racing car to handle to the satisfaction of the best drivers in the world. You might reasonably ask: "What about the tyre, surely that is a vital aspect?" Correct, but a separate subject: a good tyre will partially redeem poor suspension and good suspension will be handicapped by an inferior tyre.

Top designers are not in search of half measures or less than the best that may be achieved. That best must have at some future date things no more conceivable to us than was the electric chair to Henry VIII. The developments of the future can be of no help now. "State of the art" is still an apt if somewhat glossy description of the best at the time. Someone somewhere is forever edging it forward.
It could be you.

The 1000 b.h.p. turbocharged Grand Prix cars of the mid Eighties featured widespread use of push/pull rod suspension. The photographs show pull rod front of '84 Renault-Lotus and push rod rear of '86 Porsche/TAG-McLaren.

The Springing Medium

...springs and things

2

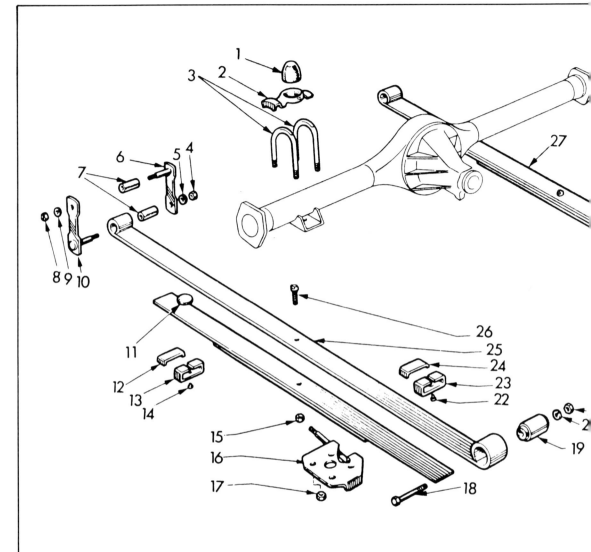

1	Rubber bump stop	8	Nut	15	Nut
2	Bump stop bracket	9	Locking washer	16	'U' bolt plate
3	'U' bolts	10	Shackle bar and stud	17	Nut
4	Nut	11	Insert	18	Bolt
5	Locking washer	12	Clamp insulator	19	Bush
6	Shackle bar and stud	13	Clamp	20	Locking washer
7	Bushes	14	Rivet	21	Nut

S uspension by definition means the vehicle is riding or hanging on something with give. It has to have some flexibility and a great deal of ingenuity has been expended on a wide variety of materials and methods of employing them over the years. As sci-fi's anti-gravity suspensors are not yet with us (though even these may appear within the lifetime of a schoolboy reader) we will examine those that are and the route that left the ubiquitous coil in the lead.

Leaf springs

This has supported and is still supporting a large part of the vehicle world from the milk float to the passenger car and commercial van and is seen on dozens of historic racing cars in our sphere. Ideas that really work are very often linked to the technology and materials existing at the time of their conception. They then become inextricably enmeshed in the industrial development of following years. The working of iron and later steel had been known to man for centuries, and technically there are great similarities between a sword or rapier blade of the first quality and the resilient leaves of a cart spring. Lay such a blade on its side with an attachment bracket of some sort at either end, tie an axle to its centre and we could be looking at a stagecoach or a Ford Escort or a Cooper Grand Prix car.

The cart spring had the early advantage of being able to be made by a blacksmith from available strips of steel and it had the incomparable plus of doing more than one job at once. This is still one aim of any good designer. The leaf spring if required located the axle in all three planes - fore and aft, side to side and when correctly tailored to its load, up and down as well. Crude as it might appear, it proved capable of very considerable refinement including multiple leaves, variable length and tapered leaves and if required even double and triple spring rate (or strength) could be achieved by differently arced leaves that only came into operation after a known amount of deflection.

The leaf spring's early use in competition appears to have pioneered at least two other refinements that had nothing to do with the quality of the metal. In the days when oil resistant rubber did not exist the springs were wrapped in neatly fitting leather gaiters filled with grease which both extended life and kept their rate constant. They could also

22 Rivet
23 Clamp
24 Clamp insulator
25 Spring leaf
26 Special bolt
27 Spring assembly

Leaf springs support the back end of the majority of road cars of all nations. This is an example of the rear leaf springs from a typical British contemporary mass-produced family car, the Ford Escort.

be tightly cord bound which tended to put the rate up, stiffening the car and, in the days when a lot of racing and sports car roadholding came from flex in the chassis, perhaps improving its performance.

Sometimes the leaf spring was transverse, trapped in the middle (Austin Seven, Ford Prefect, Cooper Formula One), sometimes it was quarter elliptic, trapped at one end while the other flexed (Austin Seven rear). But always, commercially, it was cheap despite the weight of a lot of raw material. This latter, major, handicap may yet be eliminated by the use of composite materials. Current plastic laminates research radically reduces the weight. Costs and the problem of protection from stone damage are currently keeping them off the road car, but both would be irrelevant in racing terms.

A bigger barrier is the shape of such a spring and finding the space for a really compact installation with a low centre of gravity.

Torsion bars

These are a simple length of steel tube, bar or rod, in rod form, the equivalent of a coil spring before it has been coiled. Given suitable support at each end it will twist under a given load by a precise and calculable amount. At first sight even simpler to make than the leaf spring, it cannot achieve the multiple location tasks of the leaf. This, combined with a need for a high quality material extremely closely controlled on diameter, plus bearings, end fixings and lever arms made it a relatively late starter.

Yet it is more predictable and "pure" in how it will perform, is unexposed to wear (if you don't count its molecular structure creaking and groaning and protesting) and appears easy to install. Or is it? Whether a round bar, square, laminated in strips, a tube or even a tube within a tube, it needs very strong anchor points, bearings in which to rotate and a lever of some sort through which it can be twisted under load. It does not want to contribute much to the vehicle design in other ways, and demands links all to its own to the wheels or axles.

Two main approaches to torsion bar links are generally used. With wishbones, the bar runs fore and aft and is joined (splined, clamped or welded) to the inboard end of the top or bottom wishbone. Thus the wheel may only rise or fall by twisting the bar in its length. Mounting the bar across the car

Cooper started the front to back revolution of Grand Prix car layout with a mid-engined 'special' that grew out of its early/mid Fifties 500cc racer. This example of that pioneering Single Seater shows the leaf spring suspension which was retained by the trend setting Formula One Cooper.

demands some sort of swinging link down to the axle/ wheel, whether independent or solid. All this tends to introduce complication, weight and cost. Cost horrifies the major manufacturer and weight appals the racing car builder, though the VW Beetle employed torsion bars as did Auto Union, Mercedes and Porsche though probably all due to the influence and power of Professor Porsche, but the most famous recent example has to be the Lotus approach. Colin Chapman cunningly got the tubular bar length he wanted into half the space by "doubling back" the bar to run within itself. It was a first rate example of something that, however, admirably it worked, did not permit rapid or easy alteration and was therefore of limited practicality under race pressures. While factory development engineers may well spend months getting it right for a road car, racing engineers don't have that time available. Different circuits often demand quite radical change in racing machinery: there are no "optimum settings" that will last a racing season, and spring rates are being continually varied.

Consequently, torsion bars had a short life with Team Lotus and, one might say, had no life at all when Porsche's previous commitment to bars was totally abandoned in the early Sixties for its World Championship sports prototype cars, in favour of coils all round.

The classic example of the torsion bar - VW Beetle rear suspension.
The diagram shows:
1. Axle shaft nut
2. Brake drum
3. Bearing retainer
4. Oil thrower
5. Oil seal
6. Spacer (outer)
7. 'O' ring
8. Shim washer
9. 'O' ring
10. Bearing
11. Spacer (inner)
12. Pin (locating bearing housing to tube)
13. Bearing housing
14. Bump stop bracket
15. Bump stop
16. Gaiter
17. Axle tube retainer
18. Axle tube
19. Axle shaft
20. Gasket
21. Retainer plate
22. Support bush
23. Spring plate
24. Torsion bar
25. Damper

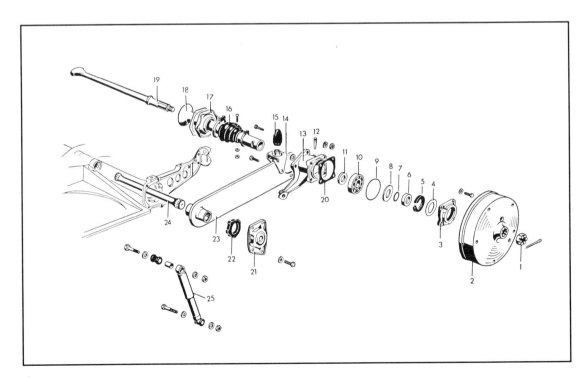

Rubber

At first sight rubber is the perfect suspension medium. It can be compact, is controllable and light for the quantity needed, with a great deal of technical know how on its employment available. But...

Hesketh had a brief flirtation using rubber blocks that were barely more than massive bump stops and soon retreated. Minis are of course the classic example but even the great Issigonis had to devise leverages of the order of 5:1 because the rubber doughnuts of Alex Moulton, despite sophisticated contours and steel inserts permitted only minimal

Mini front suspension - another classic, with rubber cone springs.
The diagram shows:
1. Lower arm pivot pin
2. Bushes
3. Locknut
4. Lower suspension arm
5. Dust cover
6. Ball-pin retainer
7. Ball-pin
8. Ball-seat
9. Spring
10. Shims
11. Lockwasher
12. Grease nipple
13. Swivel hub
14. Ring dowel
15. Steering arm
16. Lockwasher
17. Retaining plate
18. Thrust collar
19. Sealing rings
20. Upper arm pivot shaft
21. Thrust washer
22. Needle roller bearings
23. Upper suspension arm
24. Grease nipple
25. Rebound buffer
26. Bump buffer
27. Rubber cone spring
28. Cone strut
29. Spacer
30. Dust cover
31. Knuckle
32. Ball socket
33. Shock absorber
34. Upper mounting bracket
35. Upper bush
36. Sleeve
37. Distance piece
38. Locknut
39. Tie-bar
40. Tie-bar bushes
41. Cup washer
42. Locknut
The rubber cone (27) was compressed by the top suspension arm (23) through a ball-ended steel knuckle (31) and metal cone (28).

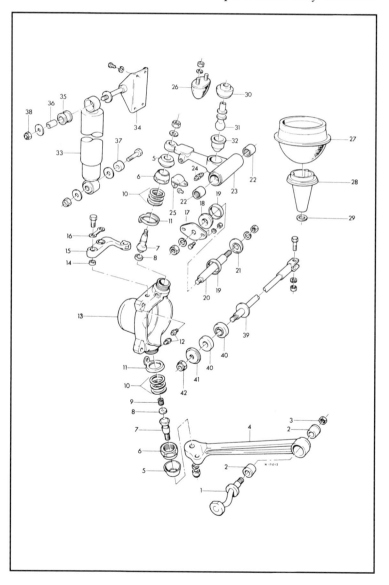

distortion. High leverages usually mean extra weight in the links and extra strength in the leverage points. Quite brilliant design (betrayed somewhat at the rear by production parts that guaranteed rust failure after a depressingly short period of time) overcame this for the Mini but an attempt by Cooper to adapt the Mini doughnuts for an early sixties Formula Junior car was barely more than a "Racing Car Show special".

Rubber has had no serious top level development, not because it would not work but probably because the steel coil spring won the battle for reasons we shall investigate in due course. It has been left to various stalwarts of the 750 Motor Club, Britain's grass roots source of almost every brain in the international race car design firmament, to employ rubber in a variety of ways. My own Terrapin Mk7 hillclimb car used Pirelli seat webbing (and Pirelli seat technology) in tension as does Reverend Barry Whitehead's RBS 4, a very successful club single seater racing car at the time of writing.

Employing rubber makes adjustment of both rate and ride height relatively simple. Using a light and adaptable wire and pulley system allows a designer to put the spring exactly where he wishes - a privilege still denied to the users of coils.

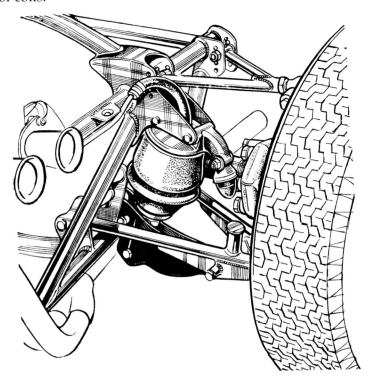

Rubber suspension, parts one and two. Early in 1963 a Cooper Formula Junior Single Seater appeared with Hydrolastic suspension (left) but the experiment was not a success. However one of the author's Terrapin single seaters used a a unique 'rubber band' rear suspension, with some success (right and overleaf).

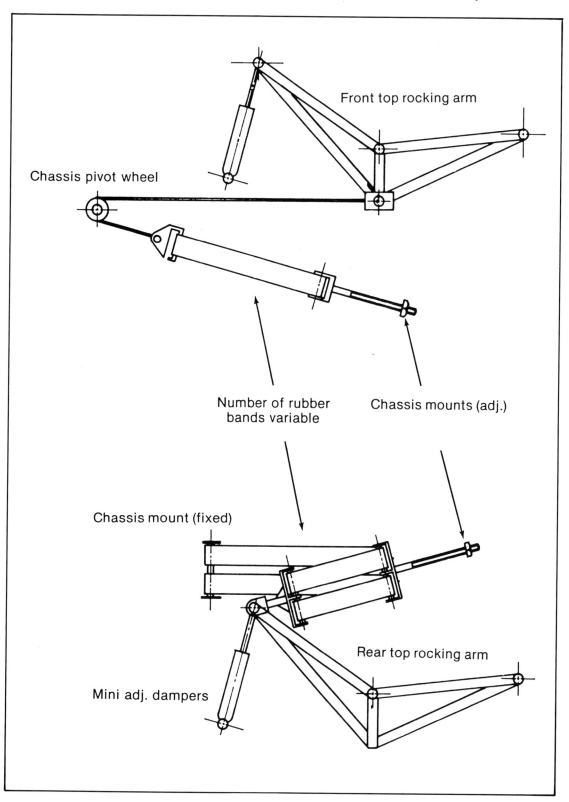

Front top rocking arm

Chassis pivot wheel

Number of rubber
bands variable

Chassis mounts (adj.)

Chassis mount (fixed)

Mini adj. dampers

Rear top rocking arm

Air

Since it is all around us and free of charge, air appears to have quite a bit going for it, and it would seem at first to be a near ideal solution to the problem of springing. It has in fact worked well in commercial applications, particularly big trucks and buses operating on bad surfaces rather than the very good roads general throughout much of Europe and the USA.

The two major shortcomings of air springs are the heat generated under continual compression and the need to keep the unit or strut containing the air topped up to the correct pressures if they are not to have variability. Air compressors, even small alloy ones, are dead weight and power stealers. Seals, piping, pistons and their operating rods, special valves all complicate the issue and add still more weight. Rubber bags, stowable under a double decker bus, pose locational difficulties in a single seater racing car.

Used as a spring, air needs damper control just like any other spring and the designer is then faced with the need for a separate yet similar unit using oil or a combined air/oil damper-cum-spring that has even more complexity and

Front suspension of the MkI BRM V16 of 1950 featured trailing arms and Lockheed air struts. Similar struts were employed at the rear, where there was a de Dion axle. Note simple ladder frame chassis.

potential for trouble. Citroen has tamed this approach for road use and such a unit was the basis of the suspension that first graced the problem-dogged BRM V16 Grand Prix car of the early Fifties. We should not ignore the fact that Bilstein use precisely this union of air and oil with great success, but in dampers which are sealed and augment a leaf or coil spring that takes the actual suspension loads and forces. All in all, air seems more trouble than it is worth at present but it is not inconceivable that future "active" suspension systems might find it has advantages over oil.

Oil

Oil has for long been the only fluid used for dampers and was adopted by Lotus to do this together with the job of the coil spring in the world's first computer controlled race car suspension system, the "Active" system regularly raced on the team's 1987 99T Grand Prix car. Proving a considerable success, active suspension represented such a mega-leap that it is dealt with fully in a complete chapter. Just like turbocharged race engines, active suspension was treated with everything from caution to derision until the day it started winning. But even before Senna's Honda-Lotus won the 1987 Monaco Grand Prix Williams publicly and McLaren privately had been at work on not dissimilar approaches, also employing oil as the springing medium.

Coil springs

So at last we come to the ubiquitous, near universal in racing coil spring. Why and how has it achieved this position of quiet superiority over every challenger after nearly a century of racing car development? The answer lies in a list of virtues that seems to go on and on - it is light, compact, inexpensive, variable in rate, length and diameter, friction free and there is a mass of knowledge concerning its manufacture and use. What more could a designer ask?

The coil spring is normally made from a high quality round steel bar with an extremely accurate outside diameter. Heated, the rod can then be wound into equal coils, tapered, given varied diameter or spacing on the coils all to achieve different results in use. Final heat treatment gives it extreme resistance against failure or deformation in use, and its reliabilty is such that it is a "fit and forget" part on literally millions of road cars.

Using the springing medium

Having chosen a springing medium, it remains to decide how best to use it and what form the spring will take; what will govern its specification be it coil, leaf, a rubber block or an oil strut governed by a computer chip. At least in its initial stages, this design problem is a relatively simple one governed by three factors:

A) The running ground clearance of the vehicle

B) The amount of suspension movement that is either required or can be tolerated

C) The wheel frequency that will provide or deal with A and B above.

Note that there has been no reference as yet to "spring rate"

Low ground clearance, as typified by the Porsche 956 Le Mans car. The all-conquering 956 featured full length ground effect venturis which run either side of a mandatory flat bottom area under the cockpit.

- perhaps the commonest term bandied about in any discussion on suspension - as this is an end result, not a starting point in any design. In itself the rate - or strength if you prefer - is meaningless as it is totally modified by two things: the sprung weight of the vehicle and the leverage exerted by the suspension.

The usual way of defining the strength of a spring in Imperial measurement is "lbs. per in.", or the weight needed to compress or deflect the spring one inch. Thus, a "150 ins./lbs." coil shortens by one inch under a load of 150 pounds. Metric units will be more familiar to many readers and are only ignored here due to the inflexibility of the author's well set mind...

While ground clearance and suspension movement or length of wheel travel are definable by anyone who can read a tape measure or ruler, wheel frequency is slightly more complex. Quoted in Cycles per Minute (CPM) or Cycles per Second (Hertz - Hz) it is the natural interval at which the

wheel (or the vehicle to which it is attached) will bounce up and down without damping or friction in the suspension mountings. It can range from 50/60 CPM for big, softly sprung saloons to 400-500 CPM for a Formula One wing car at low speed and is covered in much more detail, together with relevant formulae in Chapter Eight.

So we can now retrace our steps to A and B above. Taking ground clearance first, this has been coming down and down with every passing year. The "ultra low" racing cars of the Sixties with around 3.0" clearance look ridiculous in the Eighties when a Formula Ford car might have a setting of 1.75" at the front and 2.75" at the rear, while Formula One cars verge on 1.0" largely for aerodynamic reasons. Air flowing under the car spells trouble and drag, while discouraging the flow helps the creation of negative pressure beneath the car - downforce. So the needle noses of Formula One cars creep ever nearer the deck and the full width noses of Sports-Prototypes use splitters or scrapers as well as low clearances to help ensure that as much air as possible goes over the top rather than underneath.

Such tiny clearances dictate minimal suspension movement or the rubbing plates (or, worse still, the composite material of the tub or the rivets holding on the undertray) are all too soon seriously attacked by the tarmac as the full effect of downforce and, in the early stages, full tanks push the car nearer to the road. It is therefore clear why there are cries of distress and bitter complaint from teams when they arrive at courses with less than billiard table surfaces; particularly the American street circuits. A car designed from scratch for a specific ride height will have all sorts of problems if this has to be increased, as will become clearer in the following chapter.

Although you often see and hear the phrase "put the packers in" an increase in ride height is more usually achieved by screwing up the threaded bottom collars that lie beneath the coils. In fact, this does not affect either the spring rate or the wheel frequency as is occasionally thought but it does affect both camber, the position of the wishbones in their arcs of movement and in consequence what the wheel will do in its new position of bump and droop. And these are highly likely to be bad news for driver and team, while adding insult to injury by taking time to adjust and reset. Packers are more likely employed to limit the stroke of the damper and reduce chances of grounding. The car goes solid before hitting the ground.

Our factors A and B are two sides of the same coin. If ground clearance will permit it, the more movement that can be permitted in the spring the more the designer can vary spring rates, reduce shock loadings into the chassis or tub and increase the potential life of all the suspension components. However, if the suspension has to operate within very small wheel movement distances (as with contemporary Formula One and Sports-Prototype cars) refinements including anti-dive and rising rate will be needed to deal with the increases in loads or weight distribution under conditions of heavy braking or full tanks and these will be discussed in more detail at a later stage.

There are two other aspects of springing that come into action only when circumstances warrant it - the bump stop and the anti-roll bar. Bump stops can vary from something looking like a kitchen doorstop designed only to stop a damper closing totally and wrecking its delicate internal valving, to a most sophisticated rubber or plastic moulding

Cutaway of Spax Professional Competition Damper reveals bump stop under cone-shaped top collar. Spax' "GP" gas damper features independent adjustment for bump and rebound, which can be changed quickly and easily via the adjuster knob visible above the collar in the top mounting.

that will provide known reactions to being crushed. Naturally, it is the latter which merits, and must have, real consideration. No driver or designer wants the rate of the suspension and wheel frequency to ascend into the stratosphere or go virtually solid in tiny fractions of an inch. It

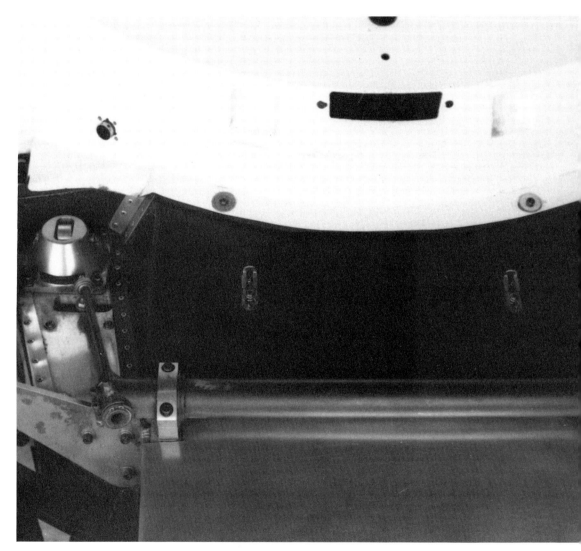

produces an instantaneous overload of the tyre on that corner and over or understeer to a gross degree.

Clearly, there is more than meets the eye to a bump stop and the two most commonly seen types are Silasto, an orangey coloured plastic foam moulding with rising rate (ie. it gets stiffer the more it is crushed) and Aeon rubbers of varying shapes, hollow moulded internally which can provide a range of differing characteristics. Other specialised companies are moving into the field, particularly as the saloon car designer has special problems with violent variations in vehicle weight and load in varying places within the wheelbase plus a high comfort requirement, making race car criteria look relatively simple.

And so to the anti-roll bar, much misunderstood because it is not only difficult to understand precisely what it is doing a lot of the time, but also is a tricky device to install well, to control and vary, and to measure when the chassis or tub to which it is attached can never be totally stiff. Indeed, the chassis may well be so lacking in rigidity that the bar will override it and contribute nothing whatever to the suspension. Given that any decent racing car should have as rigid a chassis as technically possible, the anti-roll bar will normally do nothing when the vehicle is travelling in a straight line. In a corner any vehicle will lean outwards to some degree, whether it is a 1980s Grand Prix car or a Citroen 2CV. The bar, normally a length of steel tube rather than a solid bar for weight reasons, then begins to operate.

The anti-roll bar does three things. Firstly, with its connections to the suspension on each side, it resists roll: the suspension is being asked to allow rise at the outer wheel and fall at the inner but this cannot be achieved without twisting the bar. Secondly, the bar starts acting like an extra spring added to the existing ones, particularly at the outer wheel. Thirdly, it begins moving weight off the inner tyre onto the outer one, and the combined efforts of front and rear bars can move weight off the front onto the rear, and vice versa.

What is often not realised is that the anti-roll bar is a very powerful instrument and correctly dimensioned and fitted it can provide effects five or ten times greater than simply fitting stiffer springs. It has a rate calculable in lbs./in. and the car sees it partially as an extra spring. For those wishing to fit, design or redesign an anti-roll bar there is very full explanation in Chapter Eight including methods of calculation with the necessary formulae courtesy of David Gould, the amateur designer/builder whose first honeycomb monocoque car took the British Hillclimb Championship outright in its debut season with anti-roll bars of his own calculation front and rear.

It is not always fully understood that the stiffest or most roll resistant end of the car receives the major part of any weight transfer. The weight can and does move diagonally and is the basis of "tuning" a car to handle in particular way.

The Anti Roll Bar: much misunderstood. The bar resists roll, acts like an extra spring and transfers weight. Its various effects are not always all welcome but at the front it is an almost universal fitment.

It is interesting to consider whether the recent apparent total disappearance of a rear bar from certain Formula One cars indicates they are willing to accept the major weight transfer onto the outer front wheel, in search of increased rear grip at any cost?

Leaving such detail aside, the bar for many years was considered as a simple approach to under/oversteer problems and handling balance. Too much oversteer, or a need for more understeer and you slacked the rear bar, reducing the work the outer wheel had to do and consequently its slip angle, or else you stiffened the front bar, overworked the front tyre and made it slide a little on an increased slip angle.

Cockpit-adjustable anti roll bar. The arm can be rotated by the driver via a simple linkage and is stiffest when the wide face is vertical and softest when it is horizontal. The bar mounts on the chassis and links to the suspension in the normal manner.

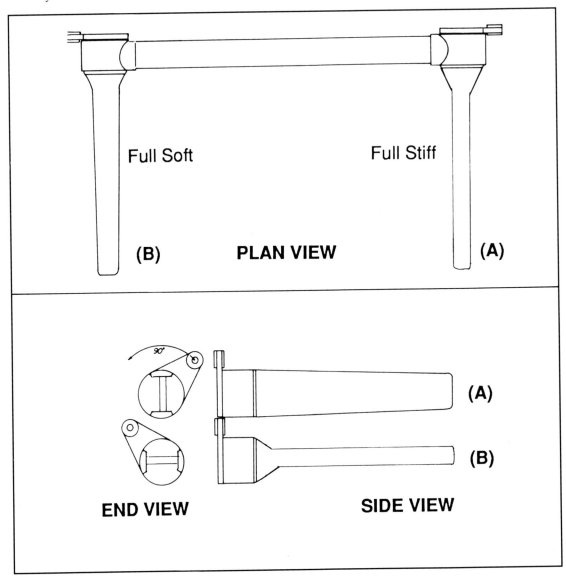

Full Soft Full Stiff

(B)   PLAN VIEW   (A)

90°

(A)

(B)

END VIEW   SIDE VIEW

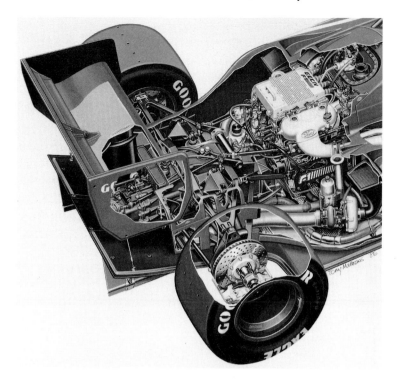

Cutaway of Cosworth/Ford-FORCE reveals compact rear anti roll bar used in conjunction with push rod suspension. This 1986 example is typical of Eighties Grand Prix car design. However, by the late Eighties a number of cars were running without rear bars for reduced weight transfer from inner to outer wheel, improving traction.

The fact that an anti-roll bar is widely employed on road cars at the front to promote understeer and less sensitivity en route to the shops (often taking the form of an integral member of the front suspension to save cost and weight) strengthens the widely held view of what it does. However, in racing the approach can well be reversed. Stiffening the front bar can cure understeer, not make it worse, and vice-versa. There seem to be at least three possible explanations for this.

Firstly, the fact that racing tyres have made giant steps in recent years means that a given car might not be fully utilising, for instance, its front tyres. To put more load into them can raise the temperature, alter the contact patch shape or pressure distribution and simply improve grip rather than reducing it. Secondly, the car may be so badly out of balance in terms of the coils and bars fitted that one end or the other is taking a totally disproportionate amount of the anti-roll resistance of the vehicle as a whole. Without knowing it in precise terms, stiffening or softening bars may simply be balancing things out and helping the suspension work properly. Thirdly, there may be an aspect of the design that means that only the bar at one end is working properly, or at all.

While it might be easy to scoff that such things are impossible at top professional level, an analysis of one such vehicle showed that 81% of the car's total roll resistance was on the back, 19% on the front. Not only did this seem wrong but massive alterations to a more equitable split transformed handling - so it can happen.

In constructional terms one might say bars began life as tubes or rods bent at from 50 - 90 degrees at each end, mounted in alloy or nylon blocks on the chassis with links down to the bottom wishbones. These links normally had a slider so that the leverage being applied to the bent end could be varied. A major step which allowed anti-roll bars to become infinitely more precise and powerful was inboard suspension - the removal of the coil to a position where it was operated within the confines of the chassis by a rocker arm of some type. What this made possible was a short, accurately dimensioned bar or tube rigidly mounted, without overhang and in proper bearings. The link to the suspension became short, convenient and permitted use of a blade adjuster.

A blade adjuster is a device of great subtlety, and of considerable difficulty to copy or assess, except by bolting them empirically to the bench and hanging a suitably calibrated spring balance on the end. The blade resembles a slice off a steel ruler. On edge it is rigid while flat it can be bent relatively easily. At intermediate positions (rotated via a spanner or a cockpit adjustable remote control) it imparts a complex variable into the basic torsional strength of the bar. The blades can be used at both ends, or singly with a non-flexible version at the opposite end. The blades are tapered, in one or both planes, and sometimes stepped in thickness. By the nature of their installation they tend to skew as well as bend under load so that what is actually happening may well be calculable, but not by me!

A simple jig bolted to a really solid bench will allow a bar to be twisted with known loads - long lever fixed to one end and bathroom scales on the other - the results being plotted onto graph paper. Doing this simple experiment with an "old fashioned" bent tube bar accorded very closely indeed with the calculated figures for its torsional stiffness. It was assumed that the bent ends were rigid, while a blade type would need a series of experiments with the blade adjusted to varying known angles.

Another aspect of the inboard linked bar is that it can be changed very conveniently and rapidly indeed. By making the outboard mountings, for instance, with a common sized

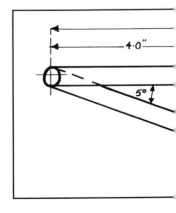

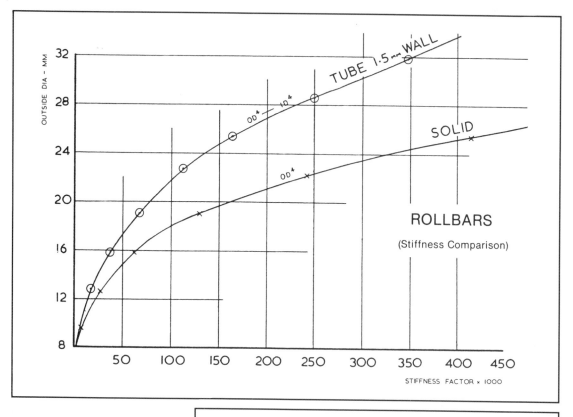

ROLLBARS

(Stiffness Comparison)

Anti roll bar twist and stiffness. Drawing left shows that five degrees of twist on an anti roll bar (or torsion) bar means different amounts of actual linear movement on a lever arm. The Graph above provides stiffness comparisions between solid and tubular bars while below is the method of calculating anti roll bar stiffness, courtesy Mike Pilbeam.

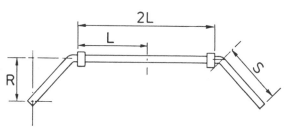

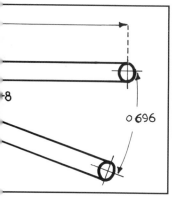

T = TRACK (INS)
K = FRACTIONAL LEVER ARM RATIO

$$\left(\frac{\text{MOVEMENT AT ANTI ROLLBAR PICKUP}}{\text{MOVEMENT AT WHEEL}}\right)$$

d = BAR DIAMETER (INS)
R = EFFECTIVE ARM LENGTH
L = HALF LENGTH OF BAR
S = LENGTH OF LEVER ARM
Q = STIFFNESS IN LB/INS PER DEGREE OF VEHICLE ROLL

$$Q = \frac{10^4 \times T^2 \times K^2 \times d^4}{R^2 \times L}$$

spigot into a small bearing a new and totally different dimensioned bar may be inserted without any other alteration. Various bars can be calculated and made at leisure, removing another unknown or variable on test. Knowing what a bar is doing, or what forces it is exerting is quite a different matter to knowing what you want it to exert, under what degree of deflection and with what relationship to its opposite number at the other end of the car.

In the broadest possible terms any vehicle will have: A) a roll couple, and B) a total roll resistance and A/B will give a theoretical roll angle in a 1G corner and for a variety of reasons the smaller the angle (probably) the better.

Formula One cars running without a rear bar also infers that some designers have obtained sufficient roll resistance from coils alone, eliminating another troublesome variable while persuading their chassis to perform well without the "fine tune" abilities of a bar. This is not as unlikely as it sounds, for an excellent and reliable guide to the handling performance of a car has, for some considerable time, been that one near its best will be sensitive to small anti-roll bar adjustments. If it requires or is not even responsive to large adjustments, something else is badly wrong, needing to be located and corrected.

As tyres have begun to take over a greater and greater part of the function of the suspension having flex and frequencies of their own (a major and separate study) they have permitted a further stiffening of springs especially on really good surfaces. Dampers, while being an integral part of any suspension system are not strictly speaking part of the springing, although a totally vital control on it, so they are covered in Chapter Seven.

So we come to "rising and falling rate" or a suspension with characteristics in the spring or linkages that cause it to become harder or softer when loads are fed in. A moment of reflection will indicate that - at least in racing - there are a number of situations in which you need things to be harder with less deflection, but very few other than emptying tanks when extra softness is required.

To be more accurate, a rising rate is aimed at either keeping the wheel frequency steady or raising it in a controlled fashion. To do this, the spring rate must be varied. Two simple examples of what happens if you do not have it are: i) under heavy braking, weight transfer onto the front wheels causes the nose of the car to be squashed down and possibly scrape on the ground; ii) downforce increases the

Gas dampers produced by Monroe with remote cylinders have been used in contempory Formula One by Williams, as shown above. Gas dampers were pioneered in Grand Prix racing by Renault working with de Carbon. Outside Formula One, Spax was a major late Eighties supplier of racing gas dampers. A plan of the Spax GP-type gas damper (as illustrated on page 43) appears right

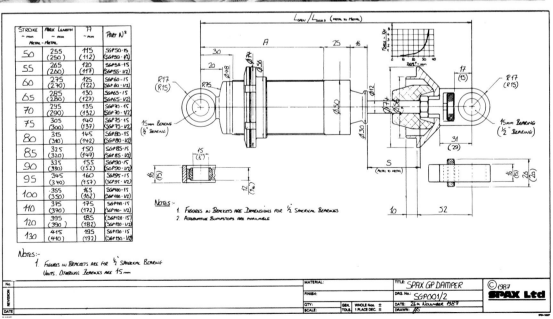

STROKE ~ mm METAL - METAL	MAX LENGTH ~ mm METAL - METAL	?? ~ mm	PART N°
50	255 (250)	115 (112)	SGP50-15 SGP50-V2
55	265 (260)	120 (117)	SGP55-15 SGP55-V2
60	275 (270)	125 (122)	SGP60-15 SGP60-V2
65	285 (280)	130 (127)	SGP65-15 SGP65-V2
70	295 (290)	135 (132)	SGP70-15 SGP70-V2
75	305 (300)	140 (137)	SGP75-15 SGP75-V2
80	315 (310)	145 (142)	SGP80-15 SGP80-V2
85	325 (320)	150 (147)	SGP85-15 SGP85-V2
90	335 (330)	155 (152)	SGP90-15 SGP90-V2
95	345 (340)	160 (157)	SGP95-15 SGP95-V2
100	355 (350)	165 (162)	SGP100-15 SGP100-V2
110	375 (370)	175 (172)	SGP110-15 SGP110-V2
120	395 (390)	185 (182)	(SGP120-15) (SGP120-V2)
130	415 (410)	195 (192)	(SGP130-15) (SGP130-V2)

NOTES:-
1. Figures in Brackets are for ½ Spherical Bearing Units. Otherwise Bearings are 15 mm

NOTES:-
1. Figures in Brackets are Dimensions for ½ Spherical Bearings
2. Alternative Bumpstops are available

15mm Bearing (½" Bearing)

R17 (R15)

R17 (R15)

15mm Bearing (½" Bearing)

L_GAN / L_?? (METAL TO METAL)

S (METAL TO METAL)

MATERIAL:		TITLE: SPAX GP DAMPER	© 1987
FINISH:		DRG. No.: SGP001/2	SPAX Ltd
QTY:	GEN. WHOLE Nos. ±	DATE: 26th November 1987	
SCALE:	TOL. 1 PLACE DEC. ±	DRAWN: B/S	

effective weight of the car, forcing it nearer the ground in a variable manner, normally linked to speed - the faster the car travels the greater the downforce and the lower it runs. In both cases suspension link movement takes place and wheel/tyre angle to the road is affected to a greater or lesser degree. And when you have Nigel Mansell on record saying that a variation of 1/8th inch in the ride height of his (1987) Williams FW11 could well be worth the gain or loss of 100lbs. of downforce, the importance of trying to stabilise ride height as far as possible is obvious.

Putting aside Lotus "Active ride", one of the paramount duties of which is to maintain a constant ride height under all conditions, much can be done through the coil, through the links or a combination of both. Taking the coil first, "rising rate" is very often "dual rate" - a simpler and poorer version. These are coils that have been more closely wound at one end in such a way that after a certain load has been applied they close up and go coilbound. The remaining coils become a shorter spring with a higher rate. The proper, more sophisticated, more difficult to calculate and manufacture and thus expensive ways are either to have coils variably wound or of taper wire. In the former case the gaps between the coils reduce bit by bit in regular increments so that one coil at a time goes solid against its neighbour, steadily reducing the effective length and increasing the rate. In the latter case the wire from which the coil is made is tapered before it is wound. The thinnest and weakest parts go coilbound first, again producing a steady increase.

A combination of a steady rate coil and a progressive bumpstop that will deal with the early, heavily loaded laps is a not uncommon compromise. And it is well to remember at the design stage that every suspension with a coil spring/ damper unit leaning inwards from the bottom wishbone has built-in falling rate with all its handicaps. Getting rid of this drawback was, initially a better argument for going inboard with rocking arms than any supposed help to the drag factor of a single seater racing car. The reason is a purely geometric one.

The forces that a bottom link can exert upwards onto the coil are at their maximum when the two are at right angles to each other. The crudest of pencil sketches will show this. But as soon as that angle begins reducing when the coil begins to lean inwards the spring suffers a steadily increasing disadvantage. It is compressed less for given wheel movement, can only exert less force because of this and is seen by the wheel as steadily weaker. The effect is very small to about 15 degrees of inclination, appreciable by 25 degrees and very seriously affecting wheel frequency by 40 degrees.

This is not to deny that the all conquering mid Eighties Porsche 956/962 Group C car employed the traditional arrangement at the front. However, Porsche fitted a very sophisticated coil with variable wind and variable wire diameter in titanium costing around $6000 a set at last enquiry, so it may well be more economic in the long run to lay out a suspension system to do the job for you.

That happens to be one advantage that pull/push rod systems offer. As they all operate through a rocker of some type to reach the coil spring/damper unit correct design, with critical angles more than 90 degrees but closing gives the spring advantage over the wheel. McLaren employed this at a very early stage but for some reason abandoned it. On balance a push rod system, if the structure of the car permits it, is likely to give fewer difficulties in achieving the objective.

The multiple Le Mans winning Porsche 956/962 mounted its spring/damper units in a vee above its transaxle and outboard at the front where it utilised progressive rate springs. Formed from titanium, these featured a variable wire diameter and a variable wind (and cost a fortune).

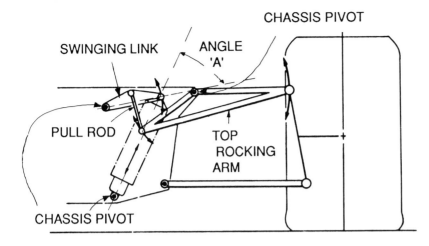

CHASSIS PIVOT

SWINGING LINK   ANGLE 'A'

PULL ROD   TOP ROCKING ARM

CHASSIS PIVOT

Unusual spring/damper mountings. The 1971 McLaren M19 featured unusual suspension linkages to provide progressive spring rate increasing with the deflection of the wheel, as the diagram (left) illustrates. The 1985 - sired Jaguar XJR-7/9 (below) mounted its spring/dampers either end of a long alloy beam, within the wheel rims, the beam spanning the ground effect tunnels.

Surrounded by rockers and variously inclined units in the world of mid Eighties Group C, ART's Tony Southgate took an elegantly simple approach at the rear when commissioned to produce a Sports-Prototype for the TWR organisation on behalf of Jaguar. The 'Jaguar XJR-7' had an alloy beam centrally mounted on the gearbox and long enough to reach to just inside each rear tyre. This was then triangulated downwards, back to the gearbox with a rod that gave a first impression that Southgate had employed a pull rod technique. He had not. Southgate mounted the spring/damper units vertically outboard, feeding the loads into the ends of the alloy beam. That gave him not only purity of motion with the minimum of trouble but also superb accessibility permitting the most rapid changes of unit, assuming only that the mechanics wear asbestos gloves for the job! While a requirement of such an approach is that the engine/gearbox unit must be able to accept the large twisting loads fed into it, the V12 block employed by TWR presumably could and did.

Location

...hanging it all on

3

"A car leans outwards on corners and attempts to throw its occupants onto the pavement" - as even Jaguar XJS racing drivers know...

Except to the most casual and uninterested observer, there is clearly more than immediately meets the eye about the way the wheel and tyre are connected to the rest of a racing car. It is invisible anyway in a Sports-Prototype unless you have an entre to the pits during practice rather than the race, and even a full and unrestricted view of a Formula One car seems to tell one barely more.

Superficially they all share remarkable similarities and some idea of what is happening once the vehicle is on the move, with the massive sideways forces of high speed cornering compressing, twisting and attempting to bend deceptively slender links, is needed if one is to have a slight appreciation of the subtleties, compromises and audacities employed.

As all drivers, spectators and aged back-seat passengers know, a car leans outwards on corners and attempts to throw its occupants onto the pavement. A full harness, wrap-round seats, and a lower centre of gravity will help make the sideways G-forces tolerable or to be ignored.

Roll angle, up to the time of writing, has not been eliminated, even in the active suspension Lotus 99T where elimination has become technically possible, as it already was with at least two designs of complex but functional linkages. Apart from such complexity being vulnerable to failure and a source of extra weight, it may be that roll, however small, is a tiny but vital part of how a driver functions, especially at the highest level of sensitivity of the dozen or so best men in the world.

Suffice to say we still have roll and its effects are fundamental to what a car does in a corner. Being a projectile that needs relatively little skill to conduct in a straight line, the corners become the key and crux of success. At the heart of it all is the roll centre. As this is both invisible and prone to move about in various ways, we will try and define it as best we may.

Looked at from head on, a cornering vehicle is not only rolling but this rotation is clearly about some point or other in space. This being a situation where a picture is worth the proverbial thousand words, the geometric and static location of the roll centre for a variety of axle links and designs, and how it is plotted are shown in the accompanying diagram.

So far, so good, but roll then begins to alter various link

angles as well as mounting point positions. These alterations can move the theoretical position of the roll centre both vertically and sideways to a greater or lesser degree.

Worse still, a plot of one side will put the roll centre in one place, and a plot of the opposite side appears to put it somewhere else. A practical (rather than mathematical or draughting) approach to what is happening to a roll centre is covered in Chapter Seven where the 'String Computer' will amuse or help the more involved reader.

However, if we accept that the roll centre cannot be in two places at once when the car has begun to roll, we appear to have a fixed geometric roll centre at rest, but a dynamic one when the vehicle is cornering that may move considerably both up and down by several inches or sideways, on occasion to some hundreds of feet - effectively infinity.

The bedrock of my own first and later suspension designs was to try and locate the roll centre as tightly as possible, keeping movement to the absolute minimum on the argument that if you did not have that as some sort of datum or starting point, what did you have? Twenty years on, it is possible both to use a computer to forecast roll centre movements, as well as, given accurate dimensions, to find out what it is doing in existing designs. What this has shown is that while the professionals have never spent much time shouting about it, they can and do take considerable trouble to locate the dynamic roll centre very well indeed, vertically in some cases within a few thousands of an inch - in practical terms, fixed. Movement of the roll centre is tied closely to roll angle, whether this be small or large and even if the car is going to roll to over 2 degrees in a 2G corner, which is more than most of us will ever experience in a lifetime, the roll centre movement and its effect on the suspension links needs to be as small and predictable as possible.

Experiment with the various layouts shortly to be considered soon showed that the various aims could not be simultaneously achieved. We can take those targets as:

a) keeping the outer or both wheels vertical in a corner, avoiding tyre lean,

b) constant track so that the tyres follow a straight line rather than a zig zag resulting from the contact patch moving in and out in sideways scrub.

c) constant camber angle thus avoiding the tyre going onto its inner edge in acceleration/braking bump or outer edge when "going light" in droop.

Only a solid axle or the lighter De Dion version appears to

Location of the static roll centre (RC) in various types of suspension. Two further cases are illustrated overleaf.

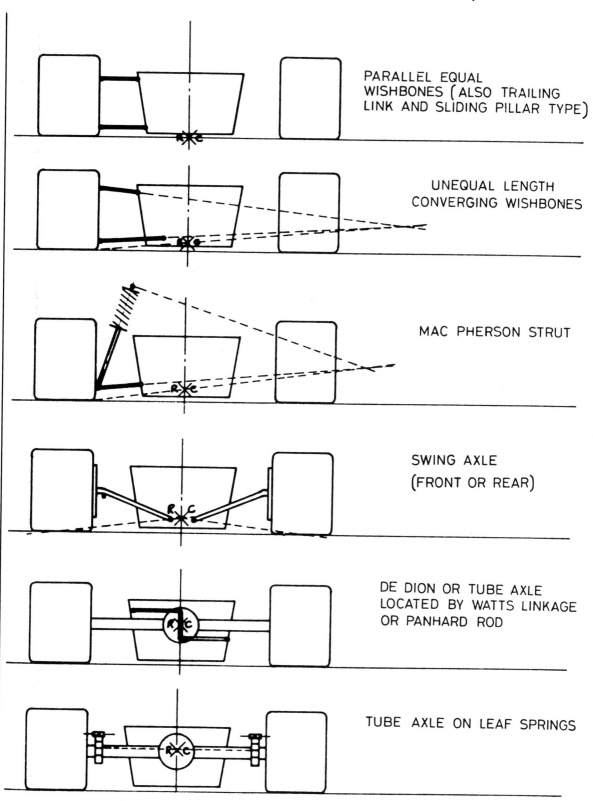

PARALLEL EQUAL
WISHBONES (ALSO TRAILING
LINK AND SLIDING PILLAR TYPE)

UNEQUAL LENGTH
CONVERGING WISHBONES

MAC PHERSON STRUT

SWING AXLE
(FRONT OR REAR)

DE DION OR TUBE AXLE
LOCATED BY WATTS LINKAGE
OR PANHARD ROD

TUBE AXLE ON LEAF SPRINGS

achieve all three aims. In practice, due to tyre distortion and weight transfer, the solid axle does not manage it either, and its weight combined with other problems means it has no place in any contemporary Formula One/Sports-Proto-type.

Attempting to achieve our three targets, it will be found that the searcher for perfection is in the middle of a triangle, trying to reach all three corners at once. As fast as he moves towards success on one, he moves away from it on the others. The first of a series of compromises will have to be made, and the three aims placed in an order of priority. Only then can a start be made to putting a dimension on the four points at each end that will dictate everything - pick ups for the upper and lower wishbones on the tub, and mounting points on the hub/upright at front and rear.

This will indicate how awkward it is, perhaps impossible, to start altering a car that has turned out badly, or gone downhill during the season. Teams could once upon a time alter brackets on a spaceframe, even on an alloy riveted tub, but pre-moulded structures with complex load paths in built are singularly unamenable to being hacked about or having extra bits glued on.

In looking at the various ways, front and rear, that have been used to suspend the racing car, there are two outside factors - one at the front and one at the rear - that complicate the issue, and influence how it can and cannot be done well.

At the front, steering with all its variable movements on

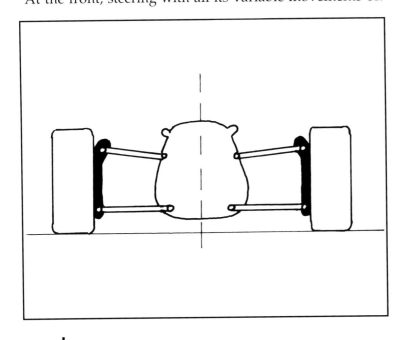

Design of the purest form of a pair of unequal length wish-bones is taken as a head on view (left) of four points. Deviations from the four (anti dive or skewed axis relative to centreline of the car) produce complex variations which need 3D computer graphics or actual car to measure, or predict.

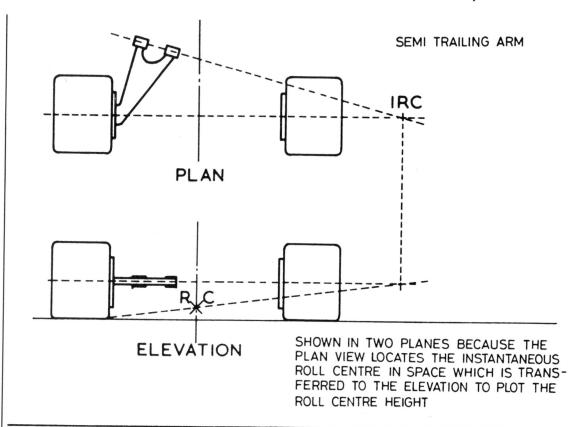

SEMI TRAILING ARM

PLAN

IRC

ELEVATION

R C

SHOWN IN TWO PLANES BECAUSE THE
PLAN VIEW LOCATES THE INSTANTANEOUS
ROLL CENTRE IN SPACE WHICH IS TRANS-
FERRED TO THE ELEVATION TO PLOT THE
ROLL CENTRE HEIGHT

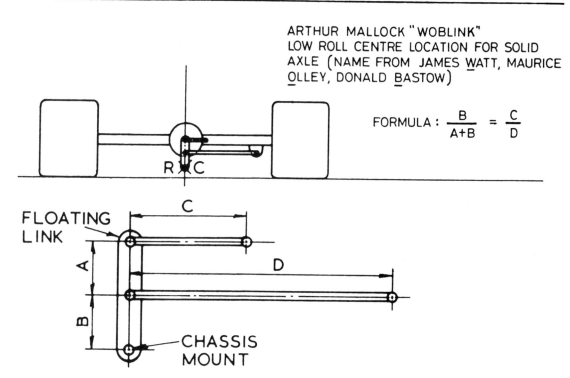

ARTHUR MALLOCK "WOBLINK"
LOW ROLL CENTRE LOCATION FOR SOLID
AXLE (NAME FROM JAMES WATT, MAURICE
OLLEY, DONALD BASTOW)

FORMULA : $\dfrac{B}{A+B} = \dfrac{C}{D}$

R C

C

FLOATING
LINK

A

D

B

CHASSIS
MOUNT

each wheel altering what should happen in an ideal situation (one wheel rising while the other falls due to caster angle, for instance). At the rear, the transfer of every scrap of power possible to the road via a contact patch at some distance from the mountings on the tub or shell, means that the links, which are also acting as the route by which forces to accelerate the car are being transferred, have a massive task quite separate from control of the wheel angle during cornering.

And both front and rear linkages need to be constructed in such a way that tiny and sensitive adjustments may be made quickly and accurately.

Front linkages

Beam axle.(on twin parallel leaf springs or a single transverse spring with radius rods or steel cables to react brake torque). Heavy, high roll centre, outer wheel leans out in corners (goes positive), movements and shocks into one wheel reacted into the other. Despite these shortcomings it was still in use in racing and on most British road cars long after America had begun to develop independent wishbones in a major way on their road cars.

Split beam. (on single transverse leaf with radius rods). Primarily this lowered the roll centre, put some static negative camber onto the wheels to compensate for going positive in roll, and was an easy and cheap means of modification to permit use of coil spring/damper units on the sports and sports/racing cars of the Fifties. It was good enough to grace a number of Chapman's Lotus models including arguably one of the greatest of them all - the beautiful, aerodynamic and hugely successful early Mk XI that came out of the Fifties.

Trailing arm.(usually with transverse torsion bar as much for ease of construction as anything). This has really only one virtue, that of a low roll centre at ground level, together with a major shortcoming - wheels assume the same angle as the vehicle in roll and there is no way of eliminating this. Nevertheless, it was used on the BRM V16 Grand Prix car and carried Aston Martin to the first and until 1987 only World Sports Car Championship victory for Britain. Used on VW Beetles, its retention is a requirement of the regulations for Formula Vee - where performance is a triumph of courage and skill over design.

Beam axle (left, on Aston Martin Le Mans car, 1933) was common pre war at the front. Professor Porsche preferred trailing arms in the Thirties as (right) on his 1936 Auto Union C-type Grand Prix car.

Leading arm. Can be seen in action on the Citroen 2CV but is frankly more at home over a French ploughed field than at Paul Ricard as it has the same shortcomings as trailing arms, plus being even less suited to angled compression loads and steering movements.

Sliding Pillar. A contemporary anachronism, to coin a phrase, which can still be seen racing on the front of the Morgan.

MacPherson Strut. A beautiful concept, which has been used in racing cars (early Lotus) and very much in rally cars of such high performance that they really count as racing cars. Has reasonably low and well controlled roll centre, but wheel angle is almost roll angle, unit is impossibly tall to fit into a really low car, and high braking forces are reacted by trying to break the unit in two and tend to lock its ability to slide in and out. Adjustment of camber and caster is far from easy. Combined with a leaf sprung driven rear axle or as front wheel drive unit it possibly equips more vehicles in the world than any alternative concept. As the Chapman Strut, seen in a non-steering rear version for the Lotus Elite and Lancia Stratos. Used on all four corners of the Toyota

MacPherson strut on Lancia Delta World Championship rally car of the late Eighties. Delta is Group A modified production car.
MacPherson struts equipped the vast majority of contemporary production cars.

LANCIA DELTA INTEGRALE GRUPPO A

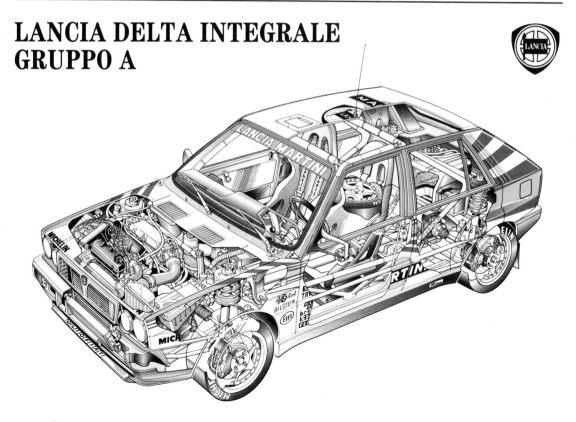

MR2 with a set of deceptively simple links that produced road handling which had every road-tester in the business searching for new superlatives.

Wishbones, equal and parallel. The roll centre is on the ground, certainly no bad thing but roll angle equals wheel angle in positive camber which we do not want. Despite this, the layout had a long lease of racing life, particularly on Cooper 500 and Cooper Bristol, using the transverse leaf spring as the top link. Not very rigid as the leaf bent sideways (ie., fore and aft) under braking and acceleration and could impart some very peculiar movements to the upright and wheel. Good bump/droop control.

Wishbones, equal and non-parallel. Can be made to give low roll centres, always helpful in reducing part of weight transfer in cornering. Flirtations in Formula One with such a layout when tubs began to get really narrow and tall at the front and when suspension movement became almost nil in ground effect era. It fitted available mounting points very conveniently and tiny suspension movement meant its geometric shortcomings we also kept small.

Wishbones, non-equal and non-parallel. Effectively the survivor everywhere because of its huge versatility. The wheel can be made to do anything the designer wishes but not, unhappily, all at the same time.

Variations on variations - wishbones come in a variety of constructions, different to look at but all still the same in principle. They can be wide based, narrow based, multi-piece with left and right-hand threaded adjusters for the benefit of caster and camber angles, and boxed or solid with

Wishbones non-parallel and non-equal: standard wear at the front of contemporary race cars. This is the Porsche/TAG-McLaren of 1986, the ultimate development by John Barnard of of his classic MP4/2 turbocar.

an inboard section to produce a rocking arm.

For reasons of weight, strength and production in advanced metals they have become ever more simple and pure in shape: a simple V in elliptical cross-section tubing to sneak the last tiny fraction of aerodynamic efficiency with a spherical joint at each corner used both top and bottom. Wishbones are also regarded as expendable being the first items to be wiped off in any accident, without damaging tub strong points, and also written off regularly, after every race in some teams, as part of a "fixed life" programme for everything on the car.

Rear linkages

Even more than at the front, a host of variations on variations during the long years of evolution to the present day.

Solid live axle. The original old faithful with a crown wheel, pinion and differential in the middle but located in a great variety of ways. Roll centre generally but not always somewhere in the centre of the differential and wheel angle mostly vertical. Too heavy and too high a roll centre for most serious racing except in the case of the Mallock U2

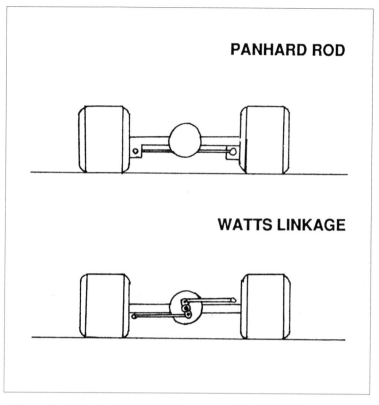

PANHARD ROD

WATTS LINKAGE

where the inimitable Major has stayed faithful, fighting a 40 year battle to keep such an axle in the fray with ever more ingenious and successful linkages to get the roll centre down and control its movements. Variously located by: leaf spring; leaf springs plus Panhard Rod; leaf/coil springs with Panhard Rod and trailing links; coils with Watt's linkage; coils, trailing arms and various Mallock arrangements; sliding centre block with leaf/coil; torque tube with leaf or coil or Panhard Rod.

De Dion. Almost as old as the car and part of all early racers. It chassis-mounts the weighty differential and drive gears while the wheels have a tube axle connecting them, keeping them vertical under all conditions unless set with negative camber during construction, as Chapman did for Formula One Vanwall. Offered the first chance of inboard brakes, a further drop in unsprung weight and brake and drive torque reacted straight into the chassis. So good that development of the Count's original, C19th version, was used by Chapman as mentioned and even a bolt-on-off version was tried by a Seventies Ferrari Formula One car. Offers choice of leaving the gearbox at the front or of making it integral with the final drive.

Classic De Dion rear end (overleaf). This is the renowned Maserati 250F Grand Prix car pictured in the works in 1954. Note transverse leaf spring and substantial radius rods.

First of the independents (left): the swing axle of the Auto Union Grand Prix car. Trailing arm front (page 65) and swing axle rear linkages gave the car poor handling and did much to spoil reputation of unusual mid-engine layout in late Thirties.

Swing axle. The first truly independently sprung driven rear wheels. Chassis mounted differential and driveshafts solid with the wheels. Looks hopeful but performs appallingly despite Professor Porsche's choice of it for the People's Wagon, the pre-War Auto Union racers and Britain's post-war Herald. High roll centre, excessive jacking with camber change, oversteer, wheels tucking under - what more do you not want? Mercedes three-quarters solved it with the well known low pivot version on the legendary 300 SLR Mille Miglia winner but other, better solutions blew it out.

Chapman strut. Colin's first solidified version of the MacPherson for rear installation. As at the front, penalised by height and far from easy adjustment, as well as a tendency to lock up under side loads.

Wishbones (or A-arms, or bottom/top links, or Z-frames) all with radius rods. Almost every variation that ingenious minds have been able to produce on the basic V of tubing with a multi-directional joint at each corner can be found on the back of some competition car somewhere. The rear has a special problem of its own, that of rear-steer, or the ability of the rear wheels, if not most carefully controlled, to alter their toe in/out angle and thus actually steering the back of the car. The forces involved particularly when the sizes and grip qualities of slick tyres began to make big steps forward rapidly became enormous.

The rear-steer forces proved capable of bending almost anything at the back of the car, of cracking chassis and gearbox casings, of tearing out their mounting points and of distorting complete rear frames. And if they couldn't break things they simply flexed the apparently inflexible. What this immediately permitted was some degree of toe-in/out to the wheel, however small. And at the rear, unlike at the front where a good driver may complain mildly but will more probably compensate almost automatically, toe in/out has a devastating effect on stability, feel and driver confidence.

Radius rods. The first move was to carry a long tube forward to a variety of mounting positions. Some gave effectively a perfect wishbone parallel to the ground and the centre line of the car, while some skewed up or down, in or out, or both. The resultant mix of arcs, pushing and pulling the rear upright here, there and everywhere produced cars that varied from good to bad to horrific.

Some designs were capable not only of causing toe in/out but also of track variation (scrub), front and backward lean and camber variation all from one bump in the road, and

Classic rear suspension of the Sixties mid-engine generation: Ferrari Grand Prix car, 1968. Note reversed lower wishbone, single upper link and upper and lower radius arms running from firewall bulkhead to upright.

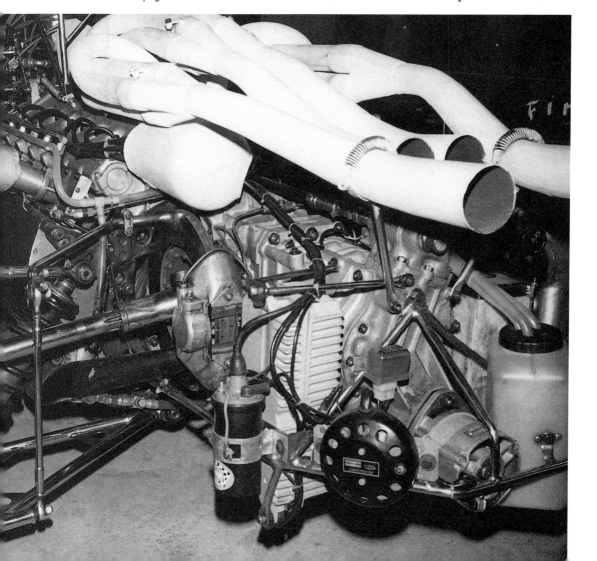

different on each side. Should anyone have needed some further complication, making the radius rods parallel and equal, equal but converging or diverging, or unequal while running uphill or downhill, produced mindboggling permutations.

One attempt to stabilise the situation a little was to use parallel bottom or top transverse links, some of which had one member which adjusted for static toe in/out. This link survived the test of time and is to be found on many current cars.

Driveshaft as one link. Lola's Eric Broadley, shortly followed by Lotus (on the 18) used this approach whereby the driveshaft carrying the power from gearbox to hub was given a second job in life as the top link while a very low mounted bottom A-frame, pointed end-in, with a radius rod did duty underneath. To complete the structure a top radius rod ran from the chassis rearward to a lug cast into the hub. Jaguar later used the system with short, compact twin double coil spring/damper units mounted on each side of the driveshaft. It worked, and does work well but from a racing point of view tied a designer to an unalterable top link with fixed length and pivot points, a finally unacceptable restriction.

The big clean-up

Designers within the car industry coming up against rear wheel steer problems were in most cases free to solve it rather brutally with skewed or inclined arms that fed in fairly violent understeer whenever the vehicle diverged from the straight and narrow. Not only were they not over concerned with the finer points, but they became responsible for the many saloon and sports cars which behaved reasonably well on the road but earned unpleasant reputations when used for competition and thus pushed really hard. Curing these shortcomings - or trying to - made the name of many a modest tuning concern, and made many a works competition manager old before his time.

In the hard worlds of Formula One and Sports-Prototype racing the problem had to be solved and perhaps the biggest pressure and influence came as a by-product of Ground Effect. Within one season it was shown that getting air out of the ever-growing side air tunnels was even more difficult than getting it in. Cluttering the air exit route were not only the driveshafts but a hotch potch of links, bars, tubes and the coil spring/damper unit, still tending to be mounted leaning inwards from the bottom wishbone. The solution, which produced the contemporary layout, featured a hefty top rocking arm, later replaced by a pull rod and linkage operating a coil spring/damper unit tucked neatly inboard beside the gearbox complete with the earlier mentioned toe-in/out link, plus a slim wide based pure V wishbone at the bottom with an outboard spherical joint that permitted camber adjustment, and made from elliptical tube. Loads went into very robust points on the engine/gearbox/tub.

Gone almost overnight were radius rods and all sorts of jointed links. When combined with truly massive cast or fabricated uprights enclosing giant hub bearings, the ability of the wheel to move other than up and down along a carefully pre-ordained path was reduced to almost nil. So elegant was the arrangement that even after venturi cars were banned, it permitted such a clean air exit at the rear of the car and on the approach to the rear wing, together with lightness, simplicity and strength that it may be some time before it is displaced.

Chassis pick-ups

Inextricably mixed with each other, suspension pick ups and their layout were influenced over the years by the steady development of the chassis, as it progressed from girders to channel to steel tube, to space frame, alloy monocoque tub, honeycomb tub, and carbon composite moulded car including stressed bodywork.

The major suspension loads emerge from the coil spring/damper units together with (in order of severity) the lower rear, the top rear, the front lower and the front top wishbones. A little reflection on how the latest tall, narrow, eggshaped outline of a current Formula One car encourages the use of a pull rod or push rod with rockers and vertical coil spring/damper rather than a top rocking arm which must have its pivots awkwardly outrigged in space in some way illustrates one example.

The loads cannot stop dead when they get to the chassis. They must be accepted with - preferably - no distortion of the structure. In a tub or chassis, rigidity combined with strength and light weight are all. Heavy chassis are a built in handicap that can never be removed, weak chassis break, usually at some critical moment, and flexible chassis defeat every single objective of the suspension designer.

Flexible chassis destroy the geometry, prevent anti roll bars working properly or at all, permit constant disputes between front and rear of the car to escalate into a war that will wreck any hopes of the vehicle ever handling properly. As with tyre technology, chassis technology is a separate and complex subject but without rigidity the suspension designer is working with both hands tied behind his back.

In accord with the unbreakable rule that you never feed a load into an unsupported tube or panel, suspension loads have tended more and more to be absorbed directly into transverse bulkheads - either cast, machined from solid, or fabricated in tube or honeycomb sheet, which are then bonded, welded or riveted into the main structure.

It is perhaps worth pointing out that the phrase "the main structure" has for many years in Formula One (though to a lesser extent in Sport-Prototypes) meant the engine and transaxle case as well as the tub. Indeed, in many categories of contemporary single seater the power unit is a fully stressed member. It is the car once you have moved aft of the rear tub bulkhead, with the front of the block being jointed to the rest of the car with methods that must provide rigidity while still accepting the expansion and contraction of the power unit from cold to full running temperature.

The block and bellhousing have to deal with major torsional stresses, and should the engine not have been conceived originally with this in mind, the likelihood of mysterious engine failure is considerable. The rear suspension pick ups tend to be on the gearbox or outriggers from it, either cast or fabricated. Looking around some cars, the unworthy thought sometimes occurs that a convenient threaded hole or flange had more to do with the location of a pick up than the required geometry.
Make a mental note to see if that car wins, ever or never.

Methods of Spring Actuation

Ideally any coil should be mounted vertically, or to be more exact at a constant 90 degrees to the lever that will compress it. A moment's reflection on the arcs involved will show that this is technically impossible with a simple linkage, but it is normally possible to keep the "lean" of the coil within plus or minus 10 degrees, or 15 degrees at worst. Within these limits, while the effective rate of the coil will be rising and falling (the dreaded "falling rate", already discussed) it will not be by an amount sufficient to cause serious trouble.

EFFECTS OF INCLINING COIL SPRING SUSPENSION UNITS.

Ideally coil springs need to be at 90 degrees to their operating mechanism and to stay as near that angle as practicable during suspension movement. When the angle alters, the effective rate of the coil alters, in most installations for the worse, giving a softening spring just when it is not wanted in bump, squat or nose dive.

Outboard, steeply inclined coils are still current under the skin of sports-prototypes, including the Porsche 962, and it is quite possible to lay out a rocking arm or push/pull rod design that will suffer from falling rate to some degree or other.

Up to 10 degrees either side of 90 degrees (ie. 20 degrees total arc) will not cause alterations worth bothering about. However, 25 degrees from the ideal rightangle is beginning to have considerable effect and 40 degrees alters things dramatically for the worse.

To obtain rising rate, the angle between the coil and its operating link needs to be more than 90 degrees and closing, or less than 90 degrees and opening. This can be very helpful in bellcrank mechanisms normally employed somewhere in push/pull rod systems.

The illustration simplifies the problem slightly (by considering the wheel as moving vertically, for instance) but will give a practical guide to the effects of inclination and angles within a suspension design.

It will be seen that although the load (100lbs.) does not alter and neither does the basic rate of the coil (100 inch/lbs.) because the chassis is moving downwards vertically while the coil swings about an arc, the chassis has to travel further than one inch to compress the coil one inch and thus reach equilibrium. When a further 150lb. of load is fed in (the bump force necessary to compress the coil a further 1.5 inches) the chassis must travel down further than a total of 2.5 inches to again reach equilibrium.

In our 40 degree example, the chassis moves down 1.376in. (a) for a static load of 100lb., with a further 2.42in. (a1) making 3.796in. for a total load of 250lb. (100lb. plus 150lb. bump).

$$\text{Effective Coil Rate (static)} = \frac{100}{1.376} = 72.67\,lb/in.$$

$$\text{Effective Coil Rate (full bump)} = \frac{250}{3.796} = 65.86\,lb/in.$$

Clearly if our design aim is a 100lb./in. coil rate we cannot get this as a constant. We can only take a rate of, say, halfway between static and full bump (ie. 69lb./in.) and work it backwards to find a coil that will give this compromise figure.

We can obtain this with the formula:

$$\frac{\text{Required rate}^2}{ECR} \quad \text{or} \quad \frac{100 \times 100}{69} = 144.9\,lb/in.$$

This coil will in fact now be harder in the static position (105.4lb./in.) and softer in full bounce (95.49lb./in.), but still a vast improvement over doing nothing and wondering why the rivet heads or exhaust system are being filed off the bottom of the car every time the brakes are applied.

How to discover the amount of vertical fall of the chassis (1.376 inches and 3.796 inches in our example) mathmatically? Use the SIN Rule formula:

$$\frac{\text{Side } a}{\text{Sin angle } A} = \frac{\text{Side } b}{\text{Sin angle } B} = \frac{\text{Side } c}{\text{Sin angle } C}$$

Note that when solving this particular problem, angle C will always be obtuse and obtuse angles do not appear in SIN tables. What you will get will be an angle somewhere between nil and 90 degrees. This angle must then be subtracted from 180 to obtain the actual angle C. Sequence:

$$\frac{\text{Side } b}{\text{Sin } B} = \frac{\text{Loaded coil length}}{\text{Sin unit angle}} = \text{Constant } K.$$

$$\text{if} \quad \frac{\text{Side } c}{\text{Sin } C} = \text{Constant } K,$$

$$\text{then} \quad \text{Sin } C = \frac{\text{Fitted coil length}}{\text{Constant } K}$$

Obtain angle C as noted above

$$\text{Angle } A = 180 - (B + C)$$

$$\text{if} \quad \frac{\text{Side } a}{\text{Sin } A} = \text{Constant } K,$$

$$\text{then} \quad \text{Side } a = K \times \text{Sin } A.$$

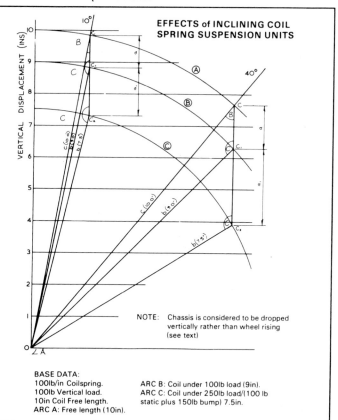

EFFECTS of INCLINING COIL SPRING SUSPENSION UNITS

NOTE: Chassis is considered to be dropped vertically rather than wheel rising (see text)

BASE DATA:
100lb/in Coilspring.
100lb Vertical load.
10in Coil Free length.
ARC A: Free length (10in).

ARC B: Coil under 100lb load (9in).
ARC C: Coil under 250lb load/(100 lb static plus 150lb bump) 7.5in.

Ignoring any spring type except the coil, currently paramount, there are three ways of utilising it.

1. Directly onto the axle, upright or wishbone. It then has to be inclined inwards to a greater or lesser degree to meet a top mounting on the tub or chassis. For many years this angle was quite large with units leaning in sometimes at 45 degrees, or even more. This not only reduces the effective rate of the spring, but causes steeply falling rate in bump. The earliest March cars took immediate steps to eliminate as much of this lean as possible by taking the top mounting as far outboard as a delicate, three-tubed support bracket would permit. Bringing the bottom mounting inwards, while apparently simpler puts very high bending loads into the bottom wishbone and also requires an ever more powerful spring because of the leverage effect, rising by a squared figure. At such extreme angles, the spring is also devoting an appreciable part of its strength to trying to pull the bottom wishbone out of the car, something we can do without.

2. Rocking arm. This was a very logical development that in one jump took the coil inboard out of the airflow, kept it more or less vertical and removed bending loads from the

To pull or to push? Modern Grand Prix cars do one or the other, sometimes both as in this case. The 1986 Honda-Williams sported pull rod rear suspension (above) and push rod front (left). This apparent lack of harmony did not stop the car winning race after race.

bottom link but at the cost of rather more difficult constructional methods and total reliance on the quality of the steel and welding.

The bearing on which the rocking arm must pivot tends to require a long expensive reaming tool or accurately machined housings to accept small self-aligning bearings and the necessary shaft and lubrication arrangements. When the wing car era was at its height coils became so strong that an appreciable part of any suspension movement came from the top rocker arms bending!

The need to thread the driver's legs between the two coils at the front placed ever greater limitations on the leverages available as cars became narrower and narrower, although the rear stayed admirably suited to this design. The coil spring/dampers are tucked neatly down beside a gearbox or clutch housing the casting often sculptured to take them. They are accessible with a low centre of gravity - and there they look like staying into the immediate future. But not at the front.

3. Push and pull rods. These opened a new era, not simply because they reduced still further, however modestly, the aerodynamic drag but they brought in a whole new era of control of when and by how much the coil was compressed by wheel movement and where it might be located. Ride height adjustment became easier and more rapid than it had ever been as the rods had left hand/right hand threaded ends. Loosening two lock nuts permitted instant alteration in length. Imponderable bending was removed, and introduction of a skewed rocker, or even a further intermediate link allowed the coil spring/damper unit to be located in a variety of situations including horizontally if required.

Technically there appears to be little or no difference between pull and push versions, both employing slim tubes of about 0.75 in., obviously of very high quality steel in perfect tension or compression. In 1987, Lotus pushed while McLaren pulled, and often the rear is different to the front and it seems considerations of space, convenience and accessibility probably govern final decisions.

If one or the other integrates more easily into certain shapes or internal design of the main structure of the car and consequent load paths that is the one that gets used. Whether front or rear the rod usually takes the loads directly out of the hub/upright through cast lugs, or alternatively via brackets welded extremely close to the ends of the top or bottom wishbone reducing outboard end bending loads to the minimum. During 1987 Williams and Benetton pushed at the front while March pulled - but either could and have altered within weeks given a powerful enough reason.

Two interesting versions of changing the direction of operation and thus placing the coil spring/damper units where it is more convenient through the use and mounting of very skilfully contrived rocker mechanisms could be seen on the front end of the 1987 Ralt Formula 3000 car and the rear end of the 1987/88 Mercedes-Sauber. The former permits the units to be located inclined in the front bay over the pedal box and hydraulic master cylinders while the latter places the units horizontally pointing forwards along the side tubes of the engine support frame.

Uprights

If any item can be called more important than others in the suspension, the upright has a good claim. At its most advanced it is a marvellous piece of design having to cope with a singularly complicated mixture of loads, stresses and strains of a very high order, the rear obviously having an

Details of the Mercedes-Sauber C8/C9 which in 1988 made a serious challenge to Jaguar's domination of the World Sports-Prototype Championship. The Sauber chassis put its spring/damper units horizontaly on its engine support frame, well away from its ground effect tunnels.

even tougher life than the front.

Among some of the criteria that must be reconciled into a shape that can be either cast or fabricated and then machined are the top and bottom suspension pick up points to accept a variety of bearings/ spherical joints, brake caliper lugs that will neither crack off nor thrust the calipers into the inner rim of the wheel, torsional and bending stiffness in vertical and horizontal planes to resist cornering, wheel and brake/acceleration forces, and bearings and oil seals that will neither disintegrate nor melt in an oven-like environment. Many also incorporate air ducting to help vented discs to function. Adjustment of toe in/out, camber and caster is usually done through whatever pattern of joint is used on the wishbones, but not always.

The Porsche 962 for one has a method at the front where the top suspension pivot and steering arm are all contained in a separately machined alloy section. This is bolted to the top of the upright with a shimmed gap. Pre-planning and design ensures that camber can be instantly adjusted by putting in or taking away shims, and the tracking of the front wheels is unaffected because the steering arm is adjusted at the same time. Crafty.

Very many front uprights have a cast-in lug to which can be bolted two horizontal alloy plates. These not only form the steering arm, but altering their size or hole locations can provide different Ackerman angles, fine bump steer adjustment and a variable steering ratio without being forced to a complete change of rack and pinion. Three separate virtues stemming from a modest addition to the shape of the casting has to be good value.

Bearings

All the suspension parts we have so far considered have to be reliably attached to each other, very often with something able to accommodate movement in three different planes. Without wishing to labour the obvious, this will be most clearly evident at the front where both the top and bottom upright joints must be capable of allowing movement for the upright to rise and fall in bump and droop and also rotate when the driver turns the steering wheel.

For very many years plain bearings of machined brass and bronze with a steel pin down the centre were the only answer, all of which suffered lubrication and anti-dirt sealing problems. Front steering rotation was achieved by a

The Porsche 956/962's top suspension pivot and steering arm are contained in a separately machined alloy section bolted to the top of the upright with a shimmed gap. Camber is adjusted by adding or removing shims without affecting tracking.

Upright and rod ends as seen on the BMW/Megatron-Ligier. Note rod end also on attachment for the underwing stay. Michel Tetu designed Ligier opts for push rod operated front and rear suspension.

king pin with bushed bearings often of top-hat form to provide a substantial thrust washer which had to deal not only with much of the weight of a front engined car, but also the instantaneous shock loads from road bumps. An alternative was a coarse Acme thread in which the front wheels actually wound themselves up and down in going round corners.

Do not think we are talking vintage or historic here. The MG to almost the last moment of its life and BL's Marina saloon of the '80s enjoyed this archaic arrangement which happens to ensure unwanted dive angle as an extra handicap. There is still a time and a place for the accurately made plain bush, its much refined son the needle roller bearing, and its cheap and versatile grandson, the plastic moulded bearing, but the first low-priced major step forward to accommodate complex motions were probably the Silentbloc and Metalastik bushes.

These bushes had a steel outer housing and steel inner sleeve with rubber bonded between the two. Variations of rubber hardness, thickness, length and diameter could provide bushes ranging from not dissimilar to bronze to types with the flexibility to suspend a delicate instrument in safety. A new generation of racing and sports car builders embraced them with enthusiasm in the Fifties. They permitted wishbones and links to move in double arcs that would have been otherwise impossible. But this very virtue ensured their days were numbered. Not, it might be said, in the motor industry in general where they became ever more sophisticated in design and application, but in racing where precision of movement became more important with every passing day.

What the industry saw as "invaluable compliance" a racing man began to see as "squidging about all over the place" and the moment the spherical joint was spotted in aircraft the days of the rubber bush were numbered. The spherical bearing or rod end is known universally and colloquially as a "Rose Joint" because Rose were not only the earliest major manufacturer in Britain but also controlled to some degree import of foreign competitors such as the German Heim variety.

There are now a number of other high quality makers including Ampep, American Uniball and Japan's NBC, all on the same principle - a ball within a ball of varying qualities of steel, various diameter bore/thread combinations, high angular movement versions, male/female,

Ampep rod ends are made by Ampep in Avon, England and are distributed to race car builders by Goldline Bearings. These bearings use Ampep's own Xi self lubricating liner system which is used in many aerospace applications.

Rod Ends

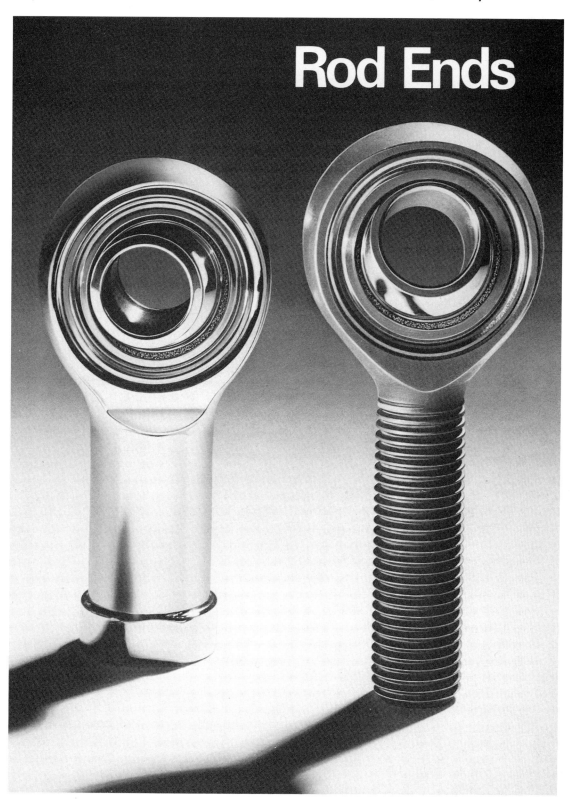

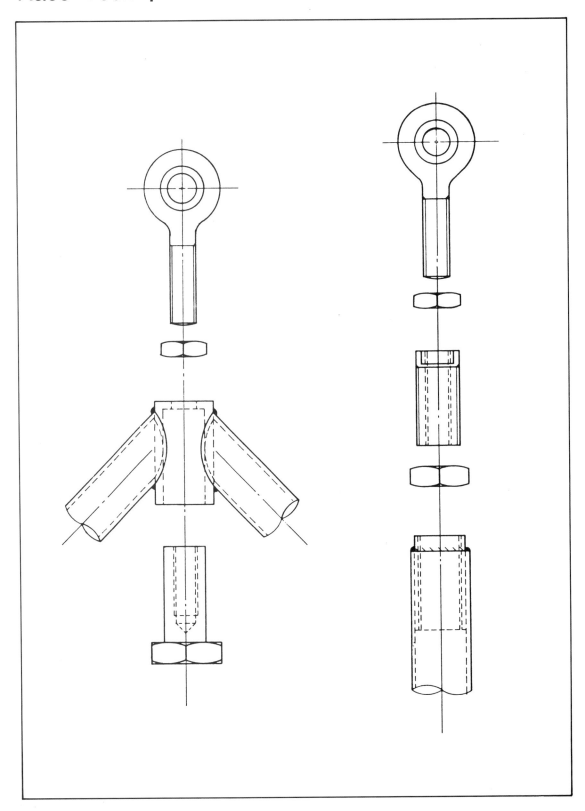

lefthand threads and right, and almost all now have a tough wear-resistant plastic woven interliner between the metal faces of inner ball and outer housing.

Spherical bearings made possible almost any variation on a suspension theme that might be envisaged by a designer. The range of sizes and materials is so wide that a compact basic guide and comparison is to be found among the Appendices.

The basic circular types are normally lightly pressed into an accurately machined housing, with a circlip of some sort making certain they stay where they have been put. Then a bolt, pin or shaft runs through the centre ball to lock it onto the other component.

Rod ends are more versatile, more easily attached by being screwed into threaded bushes and permit rapid length adjustment without dismantling by using LH and RH threads at each end of a link. In certain applications, the interliner may be more of a handicap than an advantage. The tightness it introduces through the method of manufacture, puts some amount of pre-load into the bearing - a "stiction" - which has to be overcome before the bearing will move at all, and which was incidentally a shortcoming of the moulded "Silentbloc" type of earlier rubber bush.

One example when "stiction" is certainly not wanted is the use of a large diameter bearing in the support and installation of the steering column, often running at an awkward angle, skewed in two planes relative to the car. A non-interliner pattern needs to be employed here, and a similar type is normally fitted into the ends of coil spring/damper units for similar complete freedom of movement.

Despite the high quality and variety of materials including stainless steel available "off the shelf" it is some indicator of the outlook of top level teams that they still think it worth the cost and effort to produce their own in even more exotic, aerospace-developed materials to save ounces for the same or superior strength.

As a further bonus, all the top quality units are effectively corrosion proof in a race environment, another safety and life factor.

Despite its almost universal usage and great convenience, the rod-end with its threaded shank does have the shortcoming that the shank is often required to accept bending loads, when pure compression or tension is a far more effective way of utilising the weight of metal involved.

Much thought has gone into the detail of installing spheri-

Diagram to illustrate two methods of achieving fine rod end adjustment, as described in the text.

cal bearings with ease of fine adjustment. Simple insertion into a threaded bush means no finer setting than half a turn (or half a thread) plus the need to remove the ball of the joint from its bolt or pin. March were possibly the first to produce a beautiful refinement still in widespread use, of a threaded sleeve within the main bush that can give a length adjustment literally to thousandths of an inch.

Both patterns, however, introduce a stress line into the base of one of the threads when the essential lock nut is tightened, and Tony Southgate produced his own version for the Jaguar XJR-6 where the receiving bush was split with a pinchbolt to lock the rod end. It took more time to make, lost the ultra-fine outboard adjustment but gave a tiny amount of extra strength and reliability for nothing.

A perfect view of a successful World Championship car in microcosm.

Southgate approach on extremely heavily loaded 1987 Jaguar rear suspension link to avoid locknut shear/tension loads

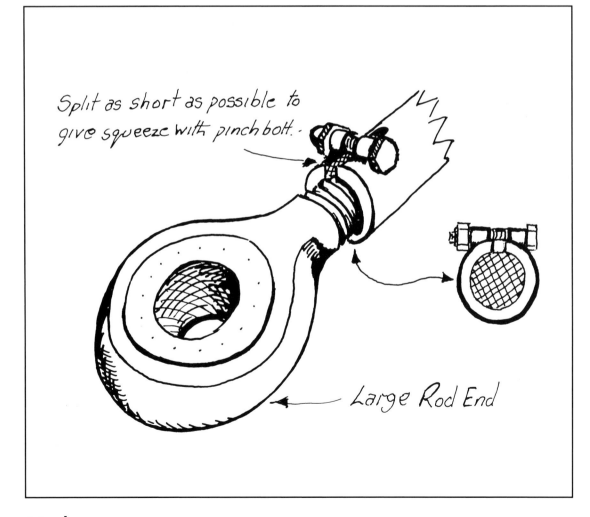

Split as short as possible to give squeeze with pinch bolt.

Large Rod End

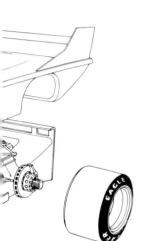

The Winning Package

...but there's always a problem

4

W hat seems to be a constant burden of the human condition - the rule that as fast as you get something right, something else goes wrong - could not be more apposite than in the situation surrounding suspension. As we have seen, there are more than enough difficulties trying to get it right in the first place, with some things that at present simply cannot be reconciled.

Having done the best we can, other parts and aspects of the car will now exert powerful effects on how it will perform, or even have to be modified in the light of actually getting out onto a track, for the track has to be a painfully different environment to the drawing office or the workshop. As the vastly experienced Brian Redman more than once has observed; "Forget what it feels like or what it looks like. What does the stopwatch say? That is the only thing that matters".

Excepting only reliability, that is a statement that brooks no argument. The points now to be considered may need fuller examination by the serious student than they are going to receive here; suspension, like any other aspect of the racing car, does not function in a vacuum. It is affected in a variety of ways once the car moves, by many of its other features, all finally coming back to the tyre contact patch.

Aerodynamics

Almost the only thing that can be said with any certainty about the airflow around a ground vehicle is that the faster it moves, the more powerful will be the effects - for good or bad. Although the earliest approaches concentrated on the concept of "streamlining" reducing drag, the only area in which this has ever seemed to achieve much success is in pure record breaking with the full teardrop shape. Mercedes' efforts with all-enveloping Formula One cars for Fangio and Moss were finally abandoned in favour of open wheel versions after showing barely measurable improvement over the open wheel version.

In the cut and thrust of normal racing, aerodynamic effects only came finally into their own with the harnessing of down-force, the reverse of the aircraft's wing lift, working through the suspension to increase tyre grip. But none of it came without the speed-sapping penalty of drag. Once regulations forbade direct mounting on the uprights, the suspension crushing force badly affected precise ride

In 1967 Chaparral shocked European road racers by appearing on the Sports-Prototype World Championship trail with this giant adjustable wing above its sophisticated Chevrolet propelled (and GM Tech-assisted) machine. The support struts fed loads directly into the uprights but wing movement and such upright mountings were subsequently outlawed.

heights and the carefully set nose down attitude that primarily controls airflow around and below the car.

At the height of the ground effect era when, as Niki Lauda has written, maximum downforce could approach 5G and a Formula One car "weighed" well over two and a half tons at 180m.p.h., suspension in the conventional and current sense simply could not cope. There were no coils or mechanisms that could deal properly with both low speeds and high so the high took precedence; coil rates of 6000lb./in. came on the scene, dampers of iron-hardness controlled the tiny movements, and "suspension" became virtually solid. What movement there was came from within the tyre carcase, itself built to provide wheel frequencies of around 400 cycles per minute, and flex in the top rockers. It was not too surprising that drivers complained of blurred vision and back trouble.

When it is realised that airflow affects the car's attitude and the car's attitude affects the airflow, the difficulties of reconciling one with another and integrating the result with the suspension will be seen more clearly, or perhaps less clearly.

Ferrari (right) was the first Grand Prix car (ahead by some hours of Brabham) to run with a rear wing: at Spa Francorchamps in 1968. Unrestricted ground effect tunnels came and went but wings remained, in 1984 sporting 'winglets' (subsequently outlawed) for extra width ahead of the axle line as allowed by the regulations and seen below on the Porsche/TAG-McLaren.

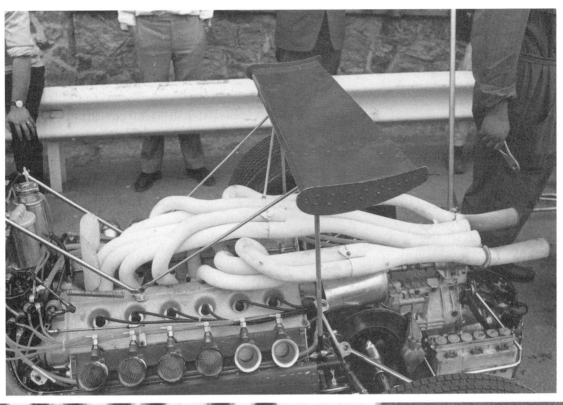

In the late Eighties downforce is still with us, in Sports-Prototypes in the fullest sense with side venturi tunnels, and in Grand Prix cars with heavily, double or triple, flapped wings, underwings and skilfully employed hot air exits from radiators, turbo aftercoolers and the exhaust pipes themselves. A full time, highly qualified (often ex-aircraft industry) aerodynamicist is now on the staff of any serious team, and those with the foresight and money already have their own wind tunnels in which to work.

But suspension has altered visibly, though movements are still small. Swing axle lengths shortened as top links altered from horizontal to a visible downward inclination towards the chassis (see Chapter Seven for a longer discourse on cause and effect of SAL). Roll has crept back to a just perceptible degree, and some slight control of the wheel in cornering has reappeared but with priority going to maintaining it vertical in bump and droop. This appears to be an overriding requirement of the tyre if it is to put 700 - 800b.h.p. on the road through two rear wheels and is highly likely to remain even with a drop to 600b.h.p. with atmospheric engines.

Uprights

The geometrical positions of the top and bottom pivots at the outboard ends are not so vital as those on the chassis, mainly because they can be integrated with the inboard ones which normally take first priority. The two main criteria are that, a) they do not contact the wheel rim - all too obvious until the day an alternative wheel or rim offset is fitted and to the consternation of one and all they foul it and begin to machine the wheel into two parts - and, b) the further outboard they can be contrived the more the leverage of the wheel against the links can be reduced.

It is certainly not unusual to see clearances so tight that specially thinned bolt heads or totally recessed cap-screws are essential.

Brakes

Over the years these drift inboard and outboard at the rear, while staying generally outboard at the front. Either way they are something of a nuisance to instal around the suspension but not serious obstacles though dissipation of the heat they generate is likely to be a different story.

Sports-Prototypes, 1970 (right) and 1985 (above) style. The '70 Porsche 917 (pictured in the wind tunnel) is a long tail special for Le Mans. Note how many of its aerodynamic features (rear fins and wing, for example) are echoed by the regular-trim Lancia LC2 15 years on.

The 1985 Renault-Tyrrell was the last Grand Prix car of recent times to run inboard rear brakes. The following year Tyrrell joined its rivals with an outboard layout for aerodynamic reasons. Note the possibly unique box-girder top wishbone.

Unsprung weight

This used to be an idol much worshipped at the expense of other things, but which has tended to sink into relative obscurity in recent years. In terms of a solid axle it is still a highly important consideration, because the sheer mass of 250/300 lbs. of steel casting, brakes, halfshafts, crown wheel and pinion, differential gears and cage puts enormous loads, strains - and thus heat generated - into dampers and mountings. However, when it is all independent, thin carcase racing tyres in combination with alloy wheels, calipers, dampers and hubs, plus carbon-carbon discs have not only massively reduced this but have also brought it down to a near "standard figure" on each corner of between 40 and 55 lbs. Any practical reduction on this makes a relatively much smaller difference to sprung weight and the consequent wheel frequency calculation is barely affected.

Carbon fibre reinforced carbon (CFRC, or carbon-carbon) disc, as supplied by AP Racing for 1986/87 Grand Prix cars. The CFRC disc was manufactured by Hitco in the USA, the company that also made Tilton carbon-carbon clutch material. Early experiments with carbon-carbon brakes by Gordon Murray of Brabham gave substantial unsprung weight advantages.

Wheels

Curious as it might sound, wheels are not really part of the suspension, except as tyre carriers, and in some areas of racing a poseur's delight. Leaving aside wood and cast iron, variations on the theme of a circle keep a mini-industry successfully in business in steel and alloy, spoked pressed, cast, one piece, in two halves and multi-section permitting variable offsets. This latter type gives the designer some elbow room in varying both the track and other clearances if desperate.

In suspension terms, wheels are nonetheless the vital link between the geometry and the tyre contact patch, and as such have to have all those old virtues - lightness, strength and reliability.

Wheels old and new. Left, a traditional Borrani wire wheel - essential equipment for Fifties World Championship cars. Right, a modern three piece Formula One wheel by Speedline. In the late Eighties slightly lighter one piece items started to replace the more versatile three-piece wheels.

Track/wheelbase ratios

Wheelbase divided by track has always had a fascination of its own, since the early days of around 2.5:1 (4 ft. track with 10 ft. wheelbase) to current karts with almost 1:1 (4 ft. track and wheelbase). Present day racing cars have tended to stabilise more because of regulations combined with the shape of a human being, the volume of 190 litres or so of fuel, an engine, oil tank and a transaxle than because there is any "perfect ratio". The increasingly widespread rule keeping the driver's feet behind the front wheel axis is a major wheelbase factor.

Given overall width maxima as well, there is very limited freedom to dispose the major components and ratios tend to be around 1.6:1 (5 ft. track with 8 ft. wheelbase). The usual restriction on track is maximum width and a reduced track is an invaluable aerodynamic help in terms of frontal area, but at a penalty in terms of roll leverage calculation, aerodynamic flow alterations and geometry restrictions. Limited freedom or not, Formula One certainly avails itself of various techniques to alter both dimensions and with them the handling of the car.

The baselines are that long slim cars have a smaller frontal area, tend towards improved stability at high speeds and are less inclined to dart about. Short, wider cars are not as fast in a straight line, are more twitchy but consequently are more sensitive and responsive on a tight course. Manoeu-

In 1986 Gordon Murray reached an all-time "high" for wheelbase/track ratio for modern Grand Prix cars with the wheelbase of his "lay-down" BMW-Brabham M12/13-.1 - BT55. The radical car boasted a 120 inch wheelbase whereas the rival, highly competitive (upright- engined) BMW-Benetton ran a 106 inch wheelbase.

vrability is partly a function of the moment of polar inertia which in turn is a function of the weight ahead of the front axle line and behind the rear and a short wheelbase helps the attainment of a low moment if the weight can still be kept within the axles.

In between these two extremes, whether handling, turn-in or speed are the priority, top drivers are as usual not only very sensitive to changes, but men of strong preference in various ways.

For these reasons if no others, methods of varying track and wheelbase without having to go away and build another car may be regarded as well worthwhile. Ferrari for one, have used alternative sets of front wishbones that moved the front wheels forward or backwards as required, and a number of teams have achieved the same result with variable length alloy spacers inserted between the engine and gearbox. Variable offset wheels, as we have seen, can alter track.

The only clear thing seems to be that there is no clear answer - yet again - or any "perfect" ratio at which to aim. More clear is that small alterations, as in so many other aspects of the design puzzle, can make major differences, for better or worse, in how a car will perform. Consequently, it will be worthwhile if at all possible to build in the ability to vary wheelbase and track, either between races, or better still while testing or in practice for an actual race.

Steering

While there have been innumerable approaches over the years, the mechanism with which the front wheels are pointed in the required direction has been distilled into a single component located in only two places. The rack and pinion, capable of great precision and infinite variation of sensitivity stands alone. As is usual in all parts that have stood the test of time, it is simple, can be made very light and strong with the correct materials and verges on 100% reliability.

From the days when it had an intermediate location somewhere between the top and bottom suspension arms, and was ahead of the driver's feet, it has finished up level with the top links, its rack-end pivots aligned exactly with the inboard pivots of the top wishbone. The only variation on this theme is that some designers put it ahead of the top suspension (Ferrari, Arrows) where it is clear of just about everything, while some place it behind (Benetton, Ligier, McLaren) where it tends to be perilously near the driver's shins.

In the latter position, it has a shorter, slightly lighter steering column, a factor instantly cancelled out if there is a need for a substantial universal joint moving through an appreciable angle, with proper support from a bearing that must itself be correctly held in an area often rather short of a suitable structure.

Should Ackerman angle be one of the aims, which in many cases it is not (though John Barnard used it with a rearward r.& p. through virtually his whole career at McLaren), the rearward location offers a much better chance of positioning the steering arm happily without it colliding with a caliper, the brake disc, or the wheel rim itself.

What even the rack and pinion cannot do is behave perfectly once the driver has begun to put on right or left lock, but unless it is giving serious bump-steer in the straight-ahead position, lesser imperfections do not appear to cause significant problems, probably dealt with by the driver automatically. Linked in with the movement of the front wheels in cornering are some implications of both the kingpin and caster angles so we shall consider them together.

1987 Cosworth/Ford-Benetton with rearward mounted steering links on push rod suspension system. Benetton had a narrow tub front with spring/dampers lying horizontal over the pedal box (ahead of the rack) to improve airflow, along with front wheel turning vanes (visible here).

King Pin Inclination (or Angle)

A useful approach to visualising what is happening during small movements in various linkages is to violently exaggerate the movement, either on paper or in your mind's eye. Contemplation of the illustrations should help clarify the following, which tends to be a bit heavy going in words alone.

Although actual King Pins are now to be seen mainly in museums, the name appears to be indestructible. That is more than can be said for the original parts which took the form of a piece of round bar, some four or five inches long and half to threequarters of an inch in diameter, gripped by heat fit or some sort of cotter in each end of a beam front axle. The hub was given two bronze bushes on which it pivoted around the pin to give steering movement to the front wheels. Lubrication and sealing against dirt frequently left much to be desired, and resulted in rapid wear.

The wear gave birth to the hallowed action by all second hand car buyers with a pretence to mechanical knowledge, of gripping the top of the front wheel for a push-pull session. All too often the wheel rocked violently in and out indicating worn pin and bushes and was a useful and potent bargaining factor. This largely irrelevant tale aside, the angle of the pin was so arranged that a line drawn through it intersected the centre line of the tyre on the road. This provided "centre point steering" with both lightness and lack of kick back through the steering wheel that is still a laudable aim, though now achieved with different and longer lived pivots.

In racing terms, the advent of ever wider tyres and the rims needed to mount them has forced a need to bury the hub ever deeper into the wheel. Accommodating a brake disc and single or twin calipers, together with the steering arm and top and bottom pivots for the wishbones, makes it even more difficult to achieve a perfect "centre point" layout.

In practice it rarely is achieved. Whether it is or not, King Pin Inclination has the more important twin effects of putting (unwanted) positive camber onto the outer wheel in a corner, together with a slight lowering of the outer wheel and thus a small but possibly important increase in its corner weight. Traditionally the inclination was of the order of 12 degrees, currently down to around 7 degrees, the less the better, down to zero were it possible to achieve "centre point" at the same time.

Caster Angle

Looking at the car in side view, the top pivot of the front upright will lie behind the lower one. The angle between the line joining these two pivots and vertical will normally be somewhere in the bracket of 2 - 6 degrees. Alternatively, the pivots are on the same vertical line but ahead of the hub - the "tea trolley" pattern. Both provide the self-centre action that helps a car run true at high speed in a straight line, and will also pull the wheels back to straight ahead coming out of a corner.

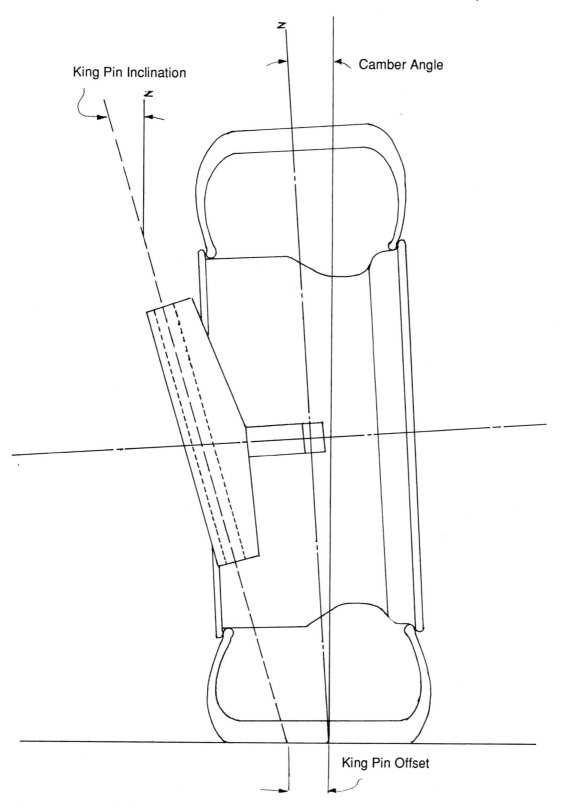

King Pin Inclination

Camber Angle

King Pin Offset

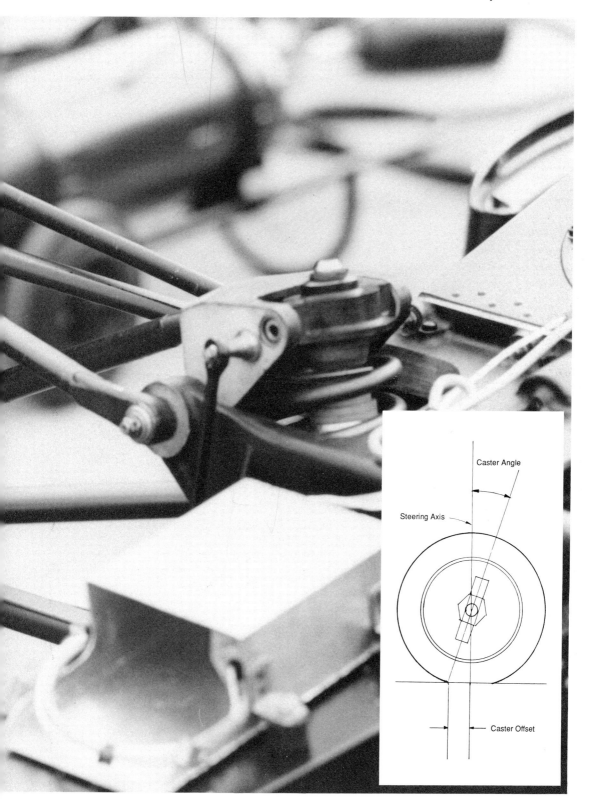

Caster Angle

Steering Axis

Caster Offset

This was well illustrated in TV pictures from Monaco when it still had the Gasworks hairpin, and a director with enough sense to put his viewers in the cockpit as drivers left the corner. Some of the cars, notably McLaren, had enough self centre to allow the drivers to simply allow the steering wheel to spin through their hands rather than indulging in a lot of cross-hands arm twirling. Nonetheless, ground effect and late Eighties cars used as little as 1 degree or on occasion nil and even "positive" caster to try and help the driver turn extremely heavy steering.

The "tea trolley" arrangement presents major difficulties in rapid alteration while the angled king pin has similar short comings to king pin inclination in that it also applies positive camber and variations in weight transfer at the outer wheel while cornering. It is essential that some form of ready adjustment be incorporated in the basic design, as, unlike in roadcars, the racing version and the drivers who will conduct it will require varying angles for varying types of circuit.

Ackerman Angle

Another example where a picture is worth a thousand words: the drawing illustrates what it is. Achieving it is easy with rear mounted racks because the steering arms will point inwards away from the wheel rim.

On various Brabham models, designer Gordon Murray also tilted the arms quite steeply uphill. This was more a convenience in the design and manufacture of the front upright than any alteration in the chosen geometry which was dictated by the final position of the track rod end.

What Ackerman provides is a reduction or avoidance of sideways "scrub" by one or other of the front tyres when turning by making the inner wheel follow a tighter circle than the outer. A moment of reflection will show that this is exactly what the tyre contact patches want to do, certainly at lower speeds. At higher velocities opinions vary, the opposition school maintaining that as the outer wheel is then carrying the majority of the weight and operating at a higher slip angle than its partner, what the inner wheel is doing or which way it is pointing becomes less and less important, to the point of irrelevance.

My own view, not solely applying to Ackerman, is that any single thing that helps the tyre contact patch to do a better job and enjoy a happier existence has to be worth any

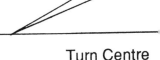

Ackerma

Turn Centre

"Full" Ackerm
of front steer
line of vehicl

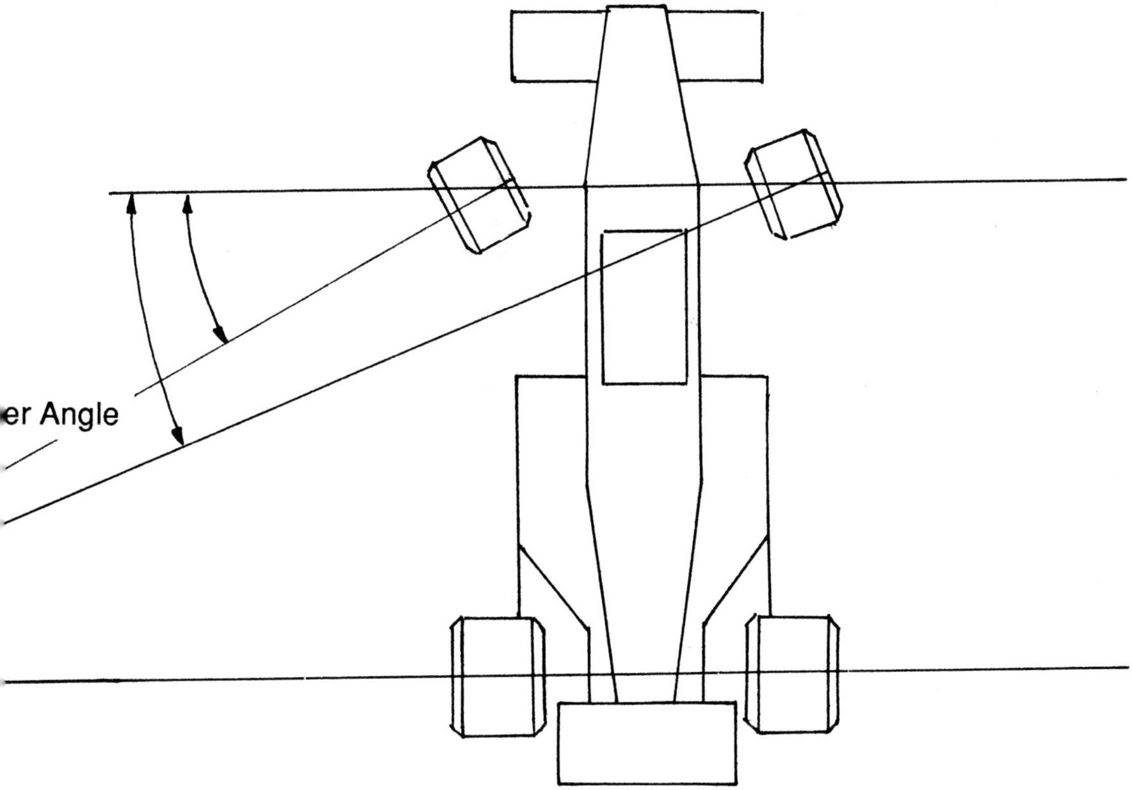

er Angle

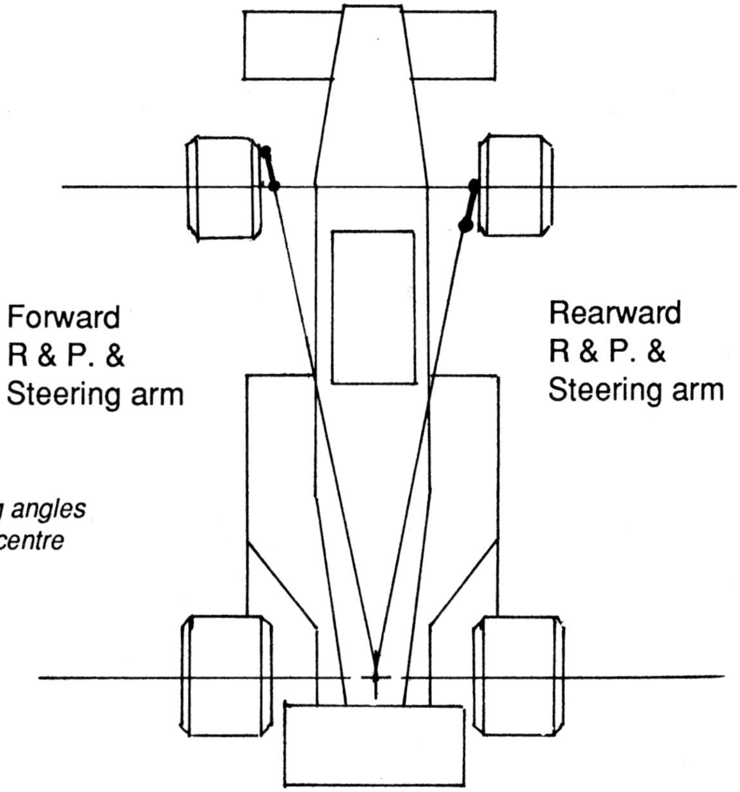

Forward
R & P. &
Steering arm

Rearward
R & P. &
Steering arm

n be reduced by altering angles
s forwards parallel with centre

trouble to achieve.

Anti Dive and Anti Squat

Without any frills, these two effects are self-explanatory in name, and are achieved by simply tilting the lines through either the front or rear wishbone chassis mounting points upwards towards the centre of the car. It is a geometric approach, as opposed to one utilising adjustment and alteration to coil springs and/or dampers, and it seems to drift in and out of fashion as the years pass by. Sometimes only anti dive will be present, preventing the nose tearing itself to pieces on the ground under heavy braking. Sometimes it will be on just the rear, hopefully helping the rear tyres avoid altering their camber angle and thus enhancing grip under acceleration.

Unfortunately, because they are geometric they are quite capable of working the wrong way when loads are reversed, and introducing very much unwanted nose or tail lift at inopportune moments.

Although illustrations, naturally enough tend to show considerable angles in search of clarity, angles in practice

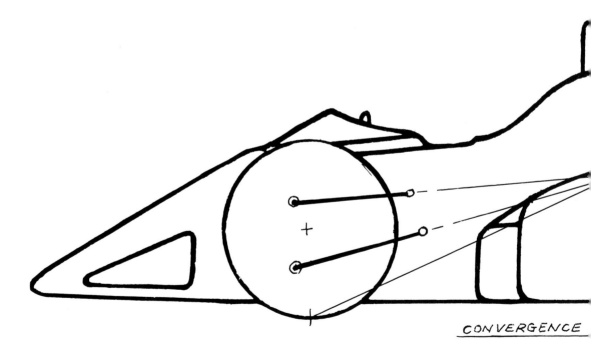

CONVERGENCE

are surprisingly small. In practical terms, we are talking about an inclination of perhaps half an inch on a base of 12 - 15 inches, or an angle of barely more than a single degree. Like many other small subtleties, whether it is being used or not, let alone to what extent, may be impossible to spot by the casual, or not-at-all casual observer.

The value of building such a facility into a suspension has, in racing terms altered a little in importance away from simply stopping things scraping on the ground to controlling the attitude of the car as closely as possible for aerodynamic reasons. During the ground effect days of the venturi cars, the angle of attack of the side pod became extremely sensitive to alteration, and the current flat-bottom cars are now almost equally sensitive to any variation in ground clearance and the exact nose-down attitude. In a sense, more sensitive as there is more suspension movement.

Both affect downforce, and consequently grip and the function of the tyre according to Sod's Law generally for the worse. While top drivers are well able to cope with smaller happenings, they are unsettling, make for less precision and smoothness, and strong complaints upon return to the pits.

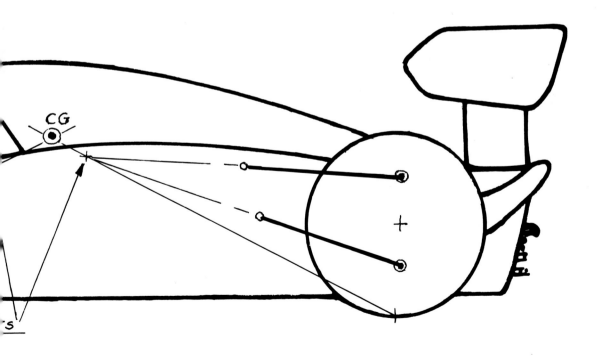

Brake Reaction Forces

Brakes are a study on their own but the forces they exert in stopping the car have to travel along the suspension links in any outboard installation - which at the front is just about every current racing vehicle. Views are divided on rear installation with strong arguments involving cooling, unsprung weight, aerodynamics and caliper mountings for both approaches.

Not only must the links or wishbones themselves be strong enough in tension and compression to hold half a ton or more decelerating from over 200m.p.h., but the loads must be fed into tub or chassis mounting points strong enough to guard against even the tiniest movement, let alone failure.

One example where it can be done to perfection with relative ease is the rear pick-up on the lower rear wishbone. These normally feed the loads either directly into the gearbox, or better still into a transverse plate or casting attached to the gearbox. Such an approach has great rigidity in all planes with a minimum of weight and complication. It can be a very different story, particularly at the front, and the solutions, some most elegant but others very definitely not, are yet another interesting paddock study.

"Stiction"

Having successfully created a near-perfect suspension in all its beauty and perfection of detail, it can be a bit depressing that once loads start feeding into it, it may not work quite as hoped.

One reason very hard to locate precisely is that the ubiquitous multi-directional spherical joint, as well as sleeve bearings rub two faces together when working. Unorthodox and unwanted resistance particularly to small movements creeps in.

Big strides in slippery, high strength plastics have allowed the use of thin interlayers (PTFE on a woven base is one example) in such bearings and has improved them vastly in terms of wear but at a certain cost in "stiction", so that designers still attempt on occasion to use a small needle roller or ball bearing if they can be sure of rotation in only one plane. It removes at least one more unknown, unless something else then flexes a few thou and produces erratically worse effects than a spherical joint could ever manage...

Apart from the suspension, "stiction" is most likely to

show itself somewhere in the steering mechanism. One tight joint, whether supporting the column rotation, in a front upright or on the end of a track rod, can produce an unpleasant dead or wooden feel that destroys any hope of driving with precision and sensitivity.

A personal test and yardstick is that with the vehicle jacked up at the front you should be able to turn the steering wheel from lock to lock with the end of the little finger bending the joints sideways. If your finger protests at this, the steering is too tight, and will have to be dismantled one joint at a time until the trouble is found. It may be that joints with no interliners (the other type always have some degree of resistance to rotation, however small) will have to be fitted before this can be eradicated. If such stiffness is left uncured, it is capable of masking a load of other problems, virtues or vices as well as any meaningful driver feedback.

Four Wheel Steering

It could be argued that this recent favourite of the ad-men has no place in this discourse on racing suspension, but such is the sophistication of the two most recent Japanese versions that its adoption by our world is far from an impossibility.

FWS has come a long way from building in roll over or understeer through the geometry of the rear links to persuade the back wheels to toe in or out in a more or less predictable fashion. Porsche devised a clever system that relied on cornering forces to distort rubber bushes in the rear suspension to produce geometric understeer in its road cars - but kept it well away from the 956/962 racers.

However, the latest approaches of Mazda and Honda both put mechanically controlled steering movements into the rear wheels. The methods are different but the aims are the same: to keep the car stable with mild understeer at high speed while giving considerable oversteer at low speed, sufficient to help parking in tight spots.

Translated into racing terms, if such movement can be inserted with delicacy and accuracy into the behaviour of the rear wheels it could be very worthwhile indeed, and is certainly in the minds of the Active suspension men. A little reflection will show that it could become an answer to the appallingly difficult problem of power understeer in racing cars with very high power combined with phenomenal rear grip. This partnership can be capable of defeating any known pair of front tyres in the appropriate circumstances, and causes designers and drivers alike endless distress, if for slightly different reasons - one trying to banish it, the other to deal with it in dangerous situations.

Path Through The Jungle ?

It should by now be crystal clear that the only hope is to try and maximise everything in a jungle of conflicting needs and aims. If a computer could give the answer it would have long since done so. Ignoring the engine, as we have done throughout, dare we define the winning formula as "Reliability, grip and handling"?

We have arrived in the mysterious and puzzling world where one car works just that tiny fraction better than another (or, in McLaren at San Marino 1988, read mega-light years better) so that it wins, even within the top group of the best-of-the-best. One area too often forgotten still lies within a designer's grasp - reliability - and the ancient law is that to win you must first finish. While you can say that this applies to every part of a racing vehicle because it carries no non-essentials, the suspension is by far the most important from the point of view of driver safety in a dangerous world and survival of the main fabric if there is trouble in testing or practice.

The suspension then has the curious double duty of not falling off under any circumstance other than one - a major off where all has gone beyond the control of the driver. When that happens it hopefully breaks off everywhere without ripping mountings and strong points in the tub. If this delicate balance of strength, weight and materials has been struck with skill, damage is kept within the bounds of immediate repair, rather than demanding a completely new car. We are speaking in terms of practice with a couple of hours or an overnight available to those unsung heros with the big Snap-On roller chests.

As well as talented design, money is a very great help to reliability. Not only does it make possible the best of materials, parts and skills, but it also permits used bits to go regularly into the scrap bin. Not following damage but on a fixed schedule of the most carefully estimated periods of time. Neglect to "life" components, or to scrupulously throw away what looks perfect after it has done a precise amount of work is one of the routes to failure or disaster.

Keeping suspension one race too many or even for more

than one race, an engine or gearbox beyond its rebuild schedule, are things not done by the serious operators. Crack testing is a way of life, and do as much in house as possible (everything?) because it permits checks and double checks and triple checks not easily carried out in somebody else's factory (unless you are Marks and Spencer, which does precisely that with every firm that supplies it with merchandise).

Grip - and more so handling - mean different things to different men and given the power and organisation of FOCA, circuits have become ever smoother reducing the need to deal with bad surfaces and their demands for large wheel movements, lower frequencies and bigger ground clearances. Hence the uproar when distant or street circuits produce ripples, surface changes, even a manhole cover or a drain to upset cars running with barely an inch ground clearance.

In recent years, approaches to grip have tended to by-pass suspension in its dynamic form, reduce its movement to the minimum and ask everything of the tyre. Ground effect achieved an increase in the "weight" of the cars of 400% and more, increasing tyre grip massively after wings had already transformed lap times, and the ill-fated Brabham fan car did the same thing. Chapman's variation on the theme with the "twin chassis" Lotus 88 met finally immovable opposition, while hydraulically adjustable suspensions for height went the same way.

It is difficult to avoid the impression that technical breakthroughs and truly innovative approaches whether in suspension or elsewhere too often meet the most violent opposition either from those who never thought of it first, or did not see quickly enough how it was admissible under the regulations. Often these ideas did not cause a ripple until they won - or were revealed by somebody with enough reputation to suggest they might well win, given a little time. Even the great Colin Chapman was not immune, opposing the Fan Car as vehemently as he defended his Twin-Chassis.

But the end result was yet again a return to at least a little suspension movement, shorter swing axle lengths, more emphasis on wheel angle, modestly reduced frequencies, all spurred on by fixed rim widths carrying control tyres. Commercial pressures far outside motor racing forced Goodyear to re-think its approach in terms of huge numbers of special qualifying tyres and endless variations introduced from race to race, and even between practice and race day.

The freedom of teams to wring small advantage from a different compound or alternative carcase was removed the day Goodyear revealed the deal that would give everybody the same tyre, with certain limits on the numbers available. The deal met with general approval, while even the critics probably felt a secret relief that the equation had been ever so slightly simplified. And the approach of very little suspension movement, high roll stiffness, cutting the ability of the car to change its attitude to the smallest limits while asking the tyre to take on a lot of the suspension task stayed at the forefront.

No-Droop Suspension

Nearing the ultimate in reduced suspension movement is a strong move towards minimal or even nil droop. It gives an effective increase in ultimate weight on the front or rear axle line or on the two inner wheels of some half the total unsprung weight - 100lbs. or more opposing roll, nose or tail lift.

This would normally stay on the ground while the coil/damper unit expanded but instead becomes an appreciable part of the equation involving weight, centre of gravity position and leverage moments. While it is a straightforward contribution to acceleration in a straight line, its effect in a corner other than on a particularly well balanced and extremely stiff car with very high roll resistance will be to lift an inner wheel in 'skewed roll'.

An even more major hazard is that astride a kerb or chicane edge the wheels can lift clear leaving the car to skid on its undertray. But it works so is being used.

These last pointers explain to a considerable extent why Lotus' Active suspension was unable to sweep the board. It was so sophisticated it could do many things that were not really needed. The things that were vital could be achieved 90% of the time with the faithful coil, hydraulic damper and steel anti-roll bar while the cost of research, experiment and a special team of experts at every race made even Formula One blanch.

The result, of course, was a parting of the ways between Team Lotus and the Group Lotus Active programme. Meanwhile, Patrick Head had taken his own mid-course and approach with what was fundamentally a self-levelling and ride height control system, hydraulically operated and with a computer "brain" issuing the orders. It was simpler, lighter, could not do a lot that Active could do - and did not need to. Piquet, whatever he said about people, said only good things about Mr Head's mechanical bits and it proved no handicap at all when despite the loss of turbo power, Mansell put it on the front row of the grid for the team's first normally aspirated outing at Rio in '88.

A pointer to everybody's future?

Active, Reactive

...the future is now (for some)

5

Senna and the Active suspension Honda-Lotus 99T: a winning combination at Monaco and Detroit........... Note the airspeed-sensing pitot head just ahead of the front wishbones, more clearly visible in the photograph on page 122.

We are now in serious danger of making the rest of this book look more like history than a useful discourse on the current state of the art on the world's quickest single seaters and sports cars. Without argument, "active" suspension is the same sort of mega-leap forward as the SU carburettor was over a bit of damp wick hanging hopefully in the inlet tract to disburse the new-fangled petroleum spirit into the entering air.

It is already, after barely eight years of admittedly intensive development, capable of vastly improving the ride, roadholding, stability and steering of even the very best of sports cars. It will alter your average car out of all recognition - like 0.9G cornering force, still the province of an extremely good competition car, from a roll-free large American saloon.

Yet mysteriously, in its most publicly visible form, in 1987 Formula One, "active suspension" by no means set the world on fire. With measured improvements in cornering speeds on the road of 10% to 15%, and needing a bare 1% superiority in Formula One to be trouncing the opposition, it appeared not yet able to achieve this.

Why not? Yet again an old adage appears valid: "The brand new will always be beaten by the last of the old - at first". A prime reason would appear to be that the contemporary alternative combination of a barely moving suspension utilising a sophisticated tyre to do much of its job, running on near perfect surfaces is able to carry out its task quite superbly. So well, in fact, that a number of the complex and difficult-to-achieve virtues of "active" are either much reduced in value or barely needed at all.

But they are certainly needed, and will transform in the coming years, railway trains, aircraft landing gear, mundane cars, trucks, buses, big earthmovers, farm tractors - virtually anything that employs the wheel.

Like carburettors before electronic fuel injection and engine management arrived, the combination of coil spring, hydraulic damper and a geometrically planned linkage for each wheel has reached an extremely refined point. But as we have seen in earlier chapters, it faces an impossible reconciliation if every aspect is to work perfectly. Wheels assume unsatisfactory angles, the frequencies of sprung and unsprung weights are hopelessly different, springs that give a comfortable ride also permit extreme roll, anti roll

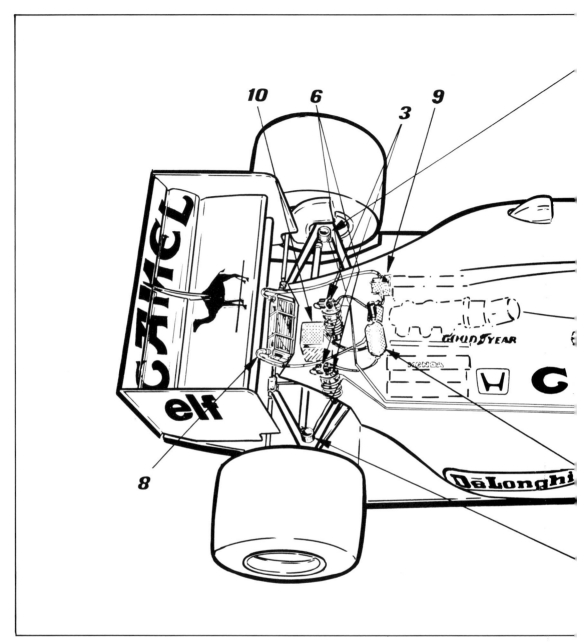

1 Pitot tubes to measure the speed of the air (taking into account car speed).
2 "Accelerometers" to measure the up and down movement of the suspension.
3 Moog servo valves to control actuator motion.
4 Two accelerometers and an inertia platform which measures the dynamics of the car (placed under driver's seat).
5 Computer brain of the car

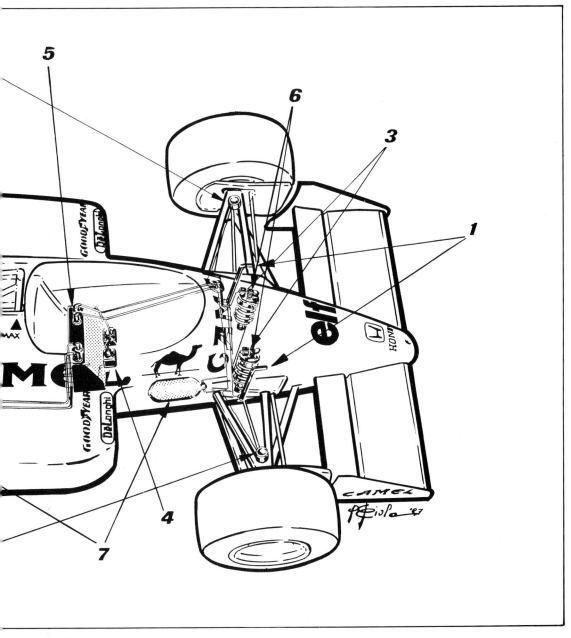

(under seat).
6 Springs to support the car
when the Active system is not
operational and to save power
when it is.
7 Accumulators to maintain
hydraulic pressure.
8 Radiator to cool hydraulic
fluid system.
9 Pump to generate hydraulic
pressure.
10 Tank for hydraulic fluid
inside gearbox.

bars helping but imperfectly.

The attractions of a "brain" that would instruct and operate a vehicle suspension, softening the ride yet stopping roll, keeping it precisely level whether under braking or the influence of a family and luggage, keeping the tyres in ideal attitudes all the time, were very great. Unsurprisingly, Lotus were very early on the scene, and currently (1988) their probably conservative guess is that they are two years ahead of the competition. Colin Chapman originally gave the go-ahead to a team of one: Lotus aerodynamicist and ground effect developer Peter Wright. The team grew to 30 and from the very first had the strongest links with the aircraft world in particular David Williams of the Cranfield institute of Technology, leader of their Flight Instrumentation Group and his team.

Fighter aircraft had already begun to enter the world where, to get the fastest possible aerobatic response, a plane was actually unstable and wanting to fall out of the sky, restrained only by a computer controlled system that balanced it until the pilot asked for action in a hurry. The situation and mechanisms required were not dissimilar to those of a Formula One car and perhaps the most vital part was a "transducer controlled actuator".

We now move into a much different vocabulary to that of conventional suspension, and without wishing to insult any reader, there is an appendix glossary for those initially unfamiliar with some of the terms, but the actuator and its operation is so fundamental to "active" that it will stand some description.

The actuator is a hydraulic ram fitted with miniature lightweight ultra-sensitive valves (made by Moog, the US company that created the music synthesiser used so widely in the pop music world) which is mounted where the coil spring/damper unit normally resides. The valves can alter its resistance to shocks and loads in tiny fractions of a second, and are controlled by the transducer. This is a device which can translate movements and their speed into electrical signals, and vice versa. It will all function so fast that the actuator becomes effectively both damper and a spring of infinitely variable rate (and, as will be seen, anti-roll bar as well).

The signals (four sets, of course, one from each wheel and all different in subtle ways) are then directed to an on-board computer and micro-processor for advice on the next move. The computer is also looking after a high pressure

USE OF THE GRID IN THE FORMULA 1 LOTUS & GTP CORVETTE ACTIVE RACE SUSPENSION

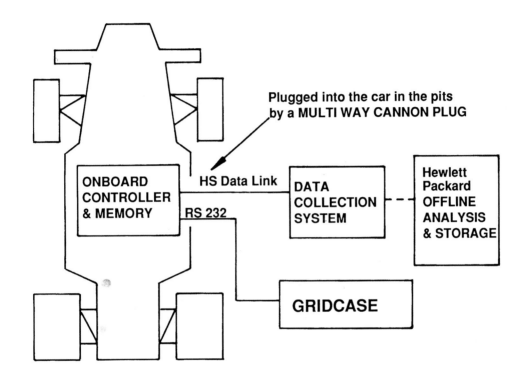

Plugged into the car in the pits
by a **MULTI WAY CANNON PLUG**

ONBOARD CONTROLLER & MEMORY

HS Data Link

RS 232

DATA COLLECTION SYSTEM

Hewlett Packard OFFLINE ANALYSIS & STORAGE

GRIDCASE

GRIDCASE
1. INITIATE DATA COLLECTION
2. ON LINE TRANSDUCER CHECKS & DIAGNOSTICS
3. CHANGE SETTINGS IN THE CONTROLLER
   (FROM KEYBOARD OR MICRO-DISC)
   EG.   STIFFNESS
         DAMPING
         HEIGHT
         HANDLING BALANCE

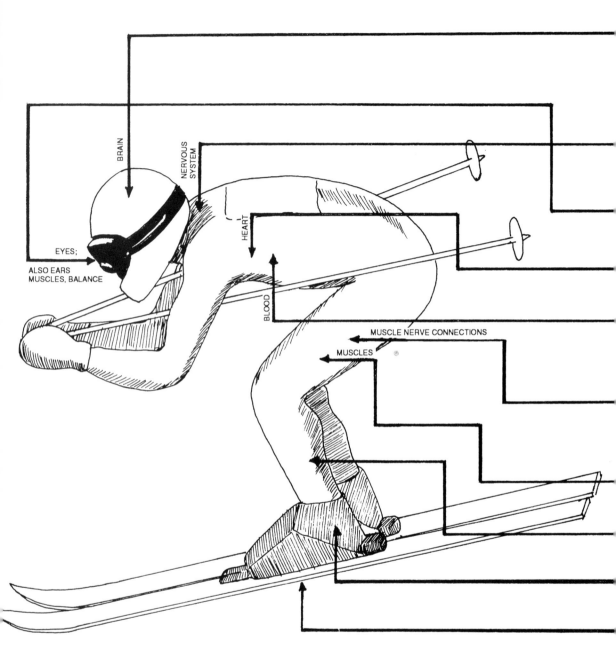

BRAIN

NERVOUS SYSTEM

HEART

EYES;

ALSO EARS
MUSCLES, BALANCE

BLOOD

MUSCLE NERVE CONNECTIONS

MUSCLES

Peter Wright's favourite analogy for Lotus' Active suspension is that it functions like a downhill skier.

The comparison is an apt one, and exhibits extraordinary similarities, as well as illustrating the prodigiously difficult task that he and his team tackled.

The complexity of a skilled human skiing downhill at high speed involves perhaps millions of messages and instructions electronically transmitted to and from the brain in ways still barely understood.

Active, while "simple" in terms of the human body, still has the same immense problem of measuring large numbers of

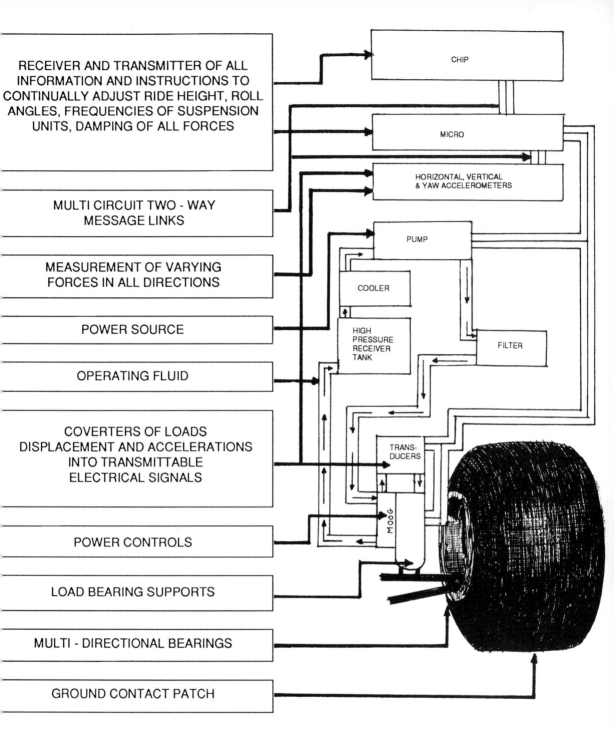

RECEIVER AND TRANSMITTER OF ALL INFORMATION AND INSTRUCTIONS TO CONTINUALLY ADJUST RIDE HEIGHT, ROLL ANGLES, FREQUENCIES OF SUSPENSION UNITS, DAMPING OF ALL FORCES

MULTI CIRCUIT TWO - WAY MESSAGE LINKS

MEASUREMENT OF VARYING FORCES IN ALL DIRECTIONS

POWER SOURCE

OPERATING FLUID

COVERTERS OF LOADS DISPLACEMENT AND ACCELERATIONS INTO TRANSMITTABLE ELECTRICAL SIGNALS

POWER CONTROLS

LOAD BEARING SUPPORTS

MULTI - DIRECTIONAL BEARINGS

GROUND CONTACT PATCH

CHIP

MICRO

HORIZONTAL, VERTICAL & YAW ACCELEROMETERS

PUMP

COOLER

HIGH PRESSURE RECEIVER TANK

FILTER

TRANS-DUCERS

MOOG

widely differing forces, central-ising that information, deciding what actions should be taken to deal with it all, and then sending the necessary instructions to the mechanisms involved to successfully control the contact patch with the ground - all in very short periods of time.

When the skier first learns to ski, he at least already has a fit, functioning electro-mechanical system complete with the most sophisticated controls: his body.

Lotus had not only to learn how to programme its equip-ment, but to create that equipment and make it work at all in the first place.

(3000p.s.i.) hydraulic pump which is delivering or accepting back oil from the actuators as they move.

If this sounds complex, it gets worse. It is not enough merely to know what the road surface, car weight and speed are doing to the wheel and tyre at each corner of the car and translating this data into electric impulses which mean something to the on-board computer. The true secret is electronically instructing those corners what to do next in a bewildering variety of situations, involving ride height, roll angle, frequencies, acceleration (or deceleration) - in fact, The Programme.

Further, human development of The Programme requires a method of recording everything that happens for later analysis and modification. Oh, and a way of altering all the controls and effects while on the move will be needed, at least in any development vehicle.

Unbelievably, the then tiny Lotus team had a crude version of all this not only built and working within months, but a Mark Two version on a Grand Prix grid within three years. The version was heavy and the Lotus 92 ran only in Brazil and Long Beach. And it did not win. But this was a fact which deceived nobody who cared to apply his mind to its future possibilities and the quality of the team driving it forward. They had given a whole new meaning to the phrase "a steep learning curve".

Consider the remarkable range of things it can already, or will very shortly achieve:

It has put springs, dampers and anti-roll bars in any conventional sense into the museum.

It has managed to beat the very best of the established Grand Prix opposition twice on the rougher street circuits of Monte Carlo and Detroit, to pick up a string of Grand Prix placings, to stick tight within the first two rows of the grid almost all year (including one pole position) and post fastest race lap twice, putting up a new record at the quick, demanding and classic home of the Italian Grand Prix - Monza. And without being unkind to the dogged and reliable Nakajima, those results were effectively achieved by one driver, Senna, in a single season.

It can maintain a steady ride height with a varying load of fuel which, if it had no other ability at all, would make it worthwhile to any Grand Prix car.

It can abolish nose-dive under braking and squat under acceleration.

It can, though nobody wants it to do so totally at the

The GM takeover of Lotus saw Active equipment appear on the Rick Hendricks run, works supported IMSA Chevrolet-Lola/Corvette Sports-Prototype at Colombus, Ohio in 1987. This is the pit equipment shipped from the UK to service the GTP machine.

moment, get rid of roll.

It does not need bump stops, corner weight adjustments, spring changes or damper alterations.

It performs all the tasks of a component that designers have dreamed of - an infinitely adjustable, sensitive and variable anti-roll bar.

And it is already able to carry out these delicate tasks despite the endlessly variable baselines of four tyre contact patches, track surfaces, weather and altitude.

Finally, it not only does them, but records what it is doing for post event analysis.

Given this torrent of proven or imminent virtues, the sane reader will not unnaturally be interested to know why Team Lotus suddenly kicked active suspension into touch after the most promising first season for a new piece of kit since Cosworth's DFV in 1967. The reasons, like those for Honda saying good-bye to the Williams team when all seemed sweetness and winners' laurel wreaths, are so obscure as to verge on incomprehensibility.

Both had superficial, one line explanations - "Toughie Frank Williams upset the Japanese by not kow-towing over drivers" and "Team Lotus could not afford to pay the bill for Active Ride (AR) technology".

Neither have much or any validity in the real world of complex deals and relationships plus the need to win at almost any cost. Like the secrets of government, shrouded for 25 or more years after the event, we may have to wait some time before the full picture in either case gets publicly pieced together.

The gossips had a field day - 'could Honda have had a hand in both affairs, responding to pressure from McLaren by laying down a condition of continued engine supply to Lotus?'

What would appear certain is that another racing car, whether in Formula One or Sports-Prototype racing, or even Team Lotus itself will return to Active when the time is right. Technical development and improvement might have its hiccoughs, but has never stopped moving forward.

Which brings us to one of the highest hurdles now faced by the creators of AR - how to sift and value the mass of information it provides to go on refining and refining The Programme.

As Peter Wright has observed, the equipment bolted onto the Lotus 99T or the Hendrick-run IMSA GTP Chevrolet-Lola/'Corvette' is not hard to see or identify. Nor are the electronic control and computer techniques any insoluble mystery to people whose job it is to understand and develop them.

The heart of the matter is being able to tell "The Brain" precisely what to do and when. The fact that Wright and his team have got so far along the road in the time they have was a key element in the decision by mega motor maker General Motors to buy Lotus lock, stock and active ride knowledge bank.

GM certainly did not buy Lotus solely to have a foot in Formula One. If the mechanisms of active suspension are banned from the Grand Prix arena, whether in the near or distant future, and there are already rumblings of such a possibility, the alternative objectives are hugely more importantly commercially and financially. The loss would be to racing, and would be a sad one.

AR will be seen in the foreseeable future on every luxury car worthy of the name. It can provide inward lean on the fastest of future railway trains. It can ensure that the weight of a vehicle picking a precarious path over rough or muddy country will stay equally distributed over each of its four - or six, or sixteen - wheels. Big trucks, fire engines, troop carriers, long distance buses and earth moving equipment can all be made to handle, ride and grip the ground in far superior ways.

Imagine the most mundane of family cars that will give a luxury ride up a farm track with the family and luggage on board. On the dash is a switch that will turn the car into a circuit racing saloon. Its general mechanisms may well be identical to a passing mechanical shovel (itself transformed in performance) with only a different master "chip" in its computer.

Such implications put Formula One firmly in its place as a good place to wave the flag, an admirable arena to force the pace of development against the hardest opposition, but sadly not essential for the survival or success of AR. They also provide a most powerful argument that the controlling powers of Grand Prix racing should not play King Canute with this or any other tide but should support the sometimes rickety contention that it is a pioneering leader in a technological world. One has to ask how future spectators would react to paying to watch racing cars that they know (even if not in technical detail) are basically inferior in a fundamental way to the vehicle they have left in the car park?

Active suspension on the 1987 IMSA GTP Corvette showing front (right) and rear suspension and some of the equipment carried in the cockpit.

AR will not initially appear on every family car for the oldest reason in the car or any other business - cost. The actuator and its valves have to be made in very large quantity, perhaps by production methods not yet devised to bring down the price, likewise the hydraulic pump, as well as the electronic controls. But anyone who doubts this may happen has only to remember that a small calculator capable or solving advanced mathematical formulae has come down from around £100 to £10 in ten years or so.

In several ways the contemporary Lotus system is still barely a half way house. In Formula One it has been "tacked on" to conventional wishbones with geometry that alters wheel angles in the course of any movement. If the car is not going to roll, trailing arms with perfect vertical wheel control could come back into their own. They were not a lot of help on the front of the ill-fated BRM V16, but that was a long time ago.

Forty years on one box under the driver's seat and two more in the side pods were accepting 28 channels of information, matching them to 80 different parameters for immediate action, and making around 250 million decisions during an average Grand Prix.

The basic approach to all this is termed by Lotus "modal control". Vehicle movement is split into four modes of wheel movement while the body is considered to stay perfectly steady. These are: a) Heave, in which all wheels rise or fall equally in relation to the body; b) Pitch, front wheels falling or rears rising, or vice-versa; c) Roll, lean to one side or the others, a motion familiar to all of us; d) Warp, a "diagonal" movement with the front "axle" tilting one way while the rear tilts the opposite.

Needless to say, there are mixtures of all of these. Each wheel possesses five channels and sends information on all of them to trigger instructions back to itself. These are: load, acceleration to the left or right, and displacement up or down.

Finally, the chassis has a further eight channels - acceleration and deceleration in three planes, lateral, longitudinal and vertical measured by suitable accelerometers, mechanical speed, and an air pressure pitot head speed crosscheck.

The hydraulic actuator at each wheel is irreversible - which means in practice it is locked solid, and the wheel cannot move until the computer has got the message(s), analysed the situation and then instructed the actuator precisely what to do with the wheel and its tyre. Depending on The Programme, the body can stay absolutely level, at a constant ride height compensating not only for a reducing fuel load, but also for the tiniest momentary tyre deflection, eliminate squat or nose dive, permit precise amounts of roll, or cause a car to roll inwards should that be thought a good idea (and currently it's not).

The function of the anti roll bar in preventing roll and, more importantly, transferring part of the car's weight from side to side and one end to another during cornering is taken over to the remarkable extent that it becomes not simply adjustable but also infinitely variable all the way through any particular corner in any manner the driver or road might demand.

As the actuator has taken over the tasks of the spring, it might well be asked what a coil is doing still visibly in situ around the unit. While it has an emergency function of supporting the car off the ground given total hydraulic failure, its primary job is to hold the car at ride height when the engine is stopped, and save the hydraulic pump the job when it is running.

As the hydraulic system does not have to do any work supporting the sprung weight there is an appreciable saving in power required to drive the 3000p.s.i. pump, and its size. Nonetheless, once the car is on the move the coil is totally under the control of the actuator.

Development has been from the beginning a classically British, semi- informal partnership. In broad (very broad) terms, Lotus do all the physical, mechanical, installation and testing work, defining what they want, while Cranfield do the electrics, having built the computer and provided the ways of doing electronically the jobs that Active required.

Says Wright: "Precisely what it does, and exactly how it does it is what we aren't telling anybody. That is our secret".

The research and testing that has already gone into it is stupendous even by Formula One terms. Not only every circuit in the world, but every corner on each of them present differing situations, all needing analysis and a corresponding set of instructions to be built into The Programme.

Power curves, wing settings and gearing have always affected handling with conventional suspension, and they haven't stopped doing so for Active. But there are much improved ways of dealing with them. The 99T had on-board facilities to record precisely what had been happening over a given period and laps. On arrival in the pits, a plug-in extractor removed the information for immediate play-back and study in the pits garage. Alterations equivalent to a complete change of coils, damper settings and roll bar size could be given to the car's Brain virtually instantaneously - no contest when measured against even the fastest, most skilled mechanics in the world.

Says Wright: "Obtaining very exact measurements is critical. We put a lot of time into this, and then the change of engine (from Renault to Honda) clouded earlier knowledge. We learned that finesse and accuracy were vital. It takes time. In total we have now run over 24,000 miles at full Grand Prix speeds. We can talk to the driver on the move. We never change anything then, but we can change up to 80 parameters at a pit stop".

On suspension geometry: "It could be argued that geometry is more important rather than less with Active. The wheels can move a great deal over bumps, be soft in heave yet very stiff in roll. Senna gave us one good example in Rio where there was one bumpy place where he had to lift off to brake in a conventional car. With the Active car he could just drive straight over it.

"It may be that the actual aims of the geometry may alter - for instance, reversing the camber change curve or different linkages that become very good if you have eliminated roll".

Another firmly entrenched view that low roll centres are imperative to reduce jacking and weight transfer but at the penalty of excessive roll would lose much of its validity if the car did not roll anyway.

Scrub, or varying track under bump/droop conditions disappears if you no longer need the particular geometry that produced it.

So, with weight cut from a starter installation of over 40kg. down to 20kg., a derisory power drain of 5b.h.p. or so from the engine, an ability to mix it with the very quickest and win - at times - it has to be asked, 'Why hasn't it wiped the floor with everybody?'

Says Wright: "I think it is because Formula One has been steadily optimised around one fundamental. It is done very much on smooth tracks with tyres, springs, roll bars and aerodynamics that have been very well developed together.

"The package has very little suspension movement and a tyre that allows that to work. We have come along with a suspension system that has to work with a tyre that is a suspension system in itself.

"We arrived at a time when all the tyres are the same - supplied by one company to everybody. We needed to change the tyre but could not. Many of the things that Active can do superbly are either not needed or not needed very badly in Formula One in its present form".

But time does not stand still. Formula One will alter, tyres will alter, company policies will alter - and Lotus' Active Suspension Group will have been toiling and advancing behind the scenes. Sooner or later they must come together again. Be ready to buy a ticket and beg a pits pass.

To be fair, such an investment is already worthwhile on the long chance that the Williams security screen might slip for a moment. Even if it did, Patrick Head's approach to suspension and the computer betrays no more than does Lotus of precisely how it works.

Visibly it appears to use conventional dampers with coils, but the centre piston rod is so massive as to indicate that it contains a part of the mechanism possibly an extremely compact hydro-pneumatic spring, normally contained - as by Citroen - in a distinctive separate sphere.

Though Williams politely but firmly refuse any technical data whatever there are two strong pointers to the system. Frank Williams has always had an undisguised loyalty to Britain and British products and brains verging on the fanatic. In 1972, Automotive Products not only produced a design for a highly sensitive, quick-acting self-leveling and no-roll system but had a prototype installed in an experimental Rover.

Further, they put it on show in Washington (USA, not the current UK home of the Japanese) and contemporary photographs show a singular resemblance to the Williams units. It was driven, as is Lotus Active, by a 3000p.s.i. pump and hydraulic system but was basically controlled by a number of pendulums which sensed horizontal and vertical G-forces and issued instructions mechanically to valves for each wheel.

Substitute accelerometers, a microcomputer and the speed of electric signalling, technology still in its infancy in ordinary industry 16 years or so ago, and the requirements of Formula One would look to have a practical answer. The AP system was noisy and cost quite a lot of money, serious handicaps in a vehicle mass market but not in racing.

As Lotus make clear, Active analyses, controls and optimises what the wheels do while the chassis is regarded as static in space. Williams looks to the other side of the coin, seeking to stabilise the body and all its aerodynamic surfaces in relation to the ground and the airflow.

The team's aerodynamicist, Frank Dernie, deeply involved from Day One, confirms the principles, if a little guardedly: "Our Reactive system was conceived to optimise the aerodynamic performance of the car as opposed to the suspension dynamics of the vehicle.

"In effect, the system is a fast load levelling device, operating in such a way that gross changes in load due to braking, cornering and aerodynamic effects give only relatively small body movements".

A short sentence covering several thousands or tens of thousands of hours work, but nontheless illuminating, bearing in mind the current static ground clearance of a F1 car of about one inch.

One other approach to roll, currently under serious development for the car industry, is inventor Cyril Mumford's answer to the question, "what does a car really need?" Given the answer, "Better ride and less roll", computer/hydraulic control of an otherwise orthodox tube or bar is a solution if it can be produced simply and cheaply enough.

Dynamic Roll Control uses hydraulic rams (what Lotus call actuators) to pre-load or stiffen the bars in a planned and progressive way as soon as the car tries to roll. The springs are totally relieved of their share of the job, and in consequence can be softer, operating at a lower and more comfortable frequency.

The computer programme needs to be able to distinguish between roll and single wheel bump, and a high pressure hydraulic pump and system operating - like Lotus and Citroen - at around 3000 p.s.i. is also needed but prototypes are up and running very successfully.

It is a vastly simpler concept than Active, and amenable to a two-step introduction to road cars - firstly to existing cars without total redesign, but then into future vehicles where it would provide freedom to use geometries at present unacceptable because of what they do in roll.

Whether it would be worth the weight, complication and power consumption in racing is still a question mark.

The Pros.

...designer suspension

6

So what happens in real life? Up to now we have been looking at suspension design construction and application, at least partly in a theoretical way.

Much of what has been spelled out is already in print, though you might have to dig energetically both to find it, and then to translate the tendencies of some academics towards florid and obscure language into simpler terms. Lest this sounds critical, it was brought on by once reading the phrase "Oversteer tendency in the non-linear handling regime." After some thought it appeared in context to mean "cornering" but it has to be unnecessary obfuscation on a stratospheric level.

Without being too sure of the relative pay rates, there are notable similarities between the racing car designer and the football manager. Both have to bring together a variety of disparate and often unpredictable things, a number of which they cannot control or forecast, working over a relatively long period. When the moment of truth or action arrives, neither can take any part of immediate consequence. Week after week, and month after month in the season, the plaudits tend to go to the stars and their undoubtedly glittering talents.

But designers and managers get one front seat for certain - the hot one at the inquest when it all goes wrong. Sometimes the situation can be retrieved in the short term, sometimes it cannot. What then comes into play is the degree of tolerance of the directors, the team managers or the sponsors. Some will accept that non-stop success is a hard act to keep going. Some will not.

Football managers would seem to hold a handsome lead in the numbers fired, payed off, or encouraged to go elsewhere. But quite a number of racing car designers have felt the same merciless pressures exerted by any sport the lifeblood of which is not just money, but money in huge amounts. Succeed or else...

And finally, the supply of the truly gifted in either sphere is strictly limited - perhaps a dozen in cars and two dozen in football, even looking worldwide. Because suspension is only one of their problems, the varying approaches and thoughts of three of the men (so far as I know, there is no women yet doing such a job) to the creation of a racing car are naturally complex. Neither Trevor Harris, nor Tony Southgate, nor Gordon Murray got the proverbial clean

Event that brought the WSPC alive: debut of the Tony Southgate-designed Jaguar XJR-6 at Mosport in 1985. Southgate is one of an extremely small group of truly gifted racing car designers active today, of whom three are interviewed here: Southgate, Trevor Harris and Gordon Murray.

sheet of paper on which to work. Motor sport has a controlling web of regulations ranging from the clarity of a stated engine capacity (1500cc seems definite enough?) to "areas licked by the airstream" and attempts to block avenues of future development almost before they get started.

Both civil and criminal law learned long ago that it is virtually impossible to use words to define all situations. Human ingenuity outwits or circumvents given the slightest chance. And if the law happens to be not only conceived in French, but written in the same language, thus demanding a translation with all the possible nuances that may or may not be read into the new version, it is not hard to see the scope for aggro and misinterpretation. Consequently, the small print of FISA usually takes precedence in first considerations of design. Any idea, however bright, must have at least a fighting chance of not getting your vehicle chucked out without ever reaching the grid.

You do not have to look very far back for excellent examples. Lotus had an epic one with its "twin chassis", which never got the chance to demonstrate the potential of its suspension; the Brabham "fan car" managed one race before going into a museum. Unrestrained ground effect tunnels and skirts survived longer, but only at the cost of the bloodiest of battles between constructors and legislators - and the rule makers won in the end.

That is to say, they won in terms of the technical specification of the cars, which had to become flat bottomed, forsaking the infinitely refined aerodynamic tunnels below the cars, but they lost their stated objective of making the cars slower. Inexplicably to the outsider, Sports-Prototypes were left free to continue with full length tunnels, making them so formidable a Jaguar XJR-8 would blow off a mid field Formula One car.

Substantial increases in the power of 1500cc turbo engines allowed much more "wing" to be dragged along by the single seater brigade with little loss of straightline speed. The downforce bonus in corners soon had everybody not only going as fast as before, but yet again slicing lap records down and down. Fairly predictably turbos got the order of the boot, in favour of engines where only Nature is allowed to push air down the inlet tracts. How long will it take "active suspension", engine management systems and power units with desmodromically operated multi valves capable of altering their opening and closing on the orders of an electronic brain, to retrieve the lost speed?

But we digress. All these are aspects of a technological explosion that has enormously increased the number of variables needing to be balanced in some way if a car has to have any chance of success at all. For obvious reasons, nobody is going to be giving away a lot of trade secrets to the world at large but some are willing to lift the veil a little on how they go about the job, their priorities in the conception of a new car, their preferred solutions to some parts of the puzzle. All have earned the utmost respect for their views the hardest way - by beating everybody else at the same game at one time or another.

Trevor Harris is 50, lives and freelances from his home in Santa Ana, California. He has worked not only in Can Am, Indy cars, Formula One and IMSA (American) Sports-Prototype racing but also in fabrication, bicycles, motor cycles and off road racers. When we met him he was doing a major project with a new IMSA car for Nissan.

The Japanese long ago sought out the talents of Harris for a top secret competition design that still lies "somewhere in Toyota's cellars" some 20 years later. Nissan came to him late in 1987 to do an IMSA GTP car that would face updated Porsche 962s and the Jaguar attack on the US series under Tom Walkinshaw.

Pundits forecasting a Jaguar-Porsche battle were more than a little shaken when Harris' Electramotive Nissan put itself on pole by two seconds at the first race, won the second at the swooping Road Atlanta from pole and the third at the tight, twisty Palm Beach, also from pole.

He had only had time to graft a new 4/5ths, including a complete new tub, onto what had already been a much modified Lola. The opposition could take no heart from his moving on to a complete new car for the season to come.

The Nissan was the latest achievement of a "great all rounder", a man who has managed to earn a living in design since he was 22 with ideas that include exhaust manifolds, aerodynamics, an infinitely variable gear for a pedal cycle which for a time financed his racing, the tiny wheeled Frisbee Can Am, Indy Cars, Shadow Formula One, making chassis, uprights and wishbones with his own hands.

Harris reflects the immense variety of motorsport in America, compared to a European tendency to focus on single seaters and Formula One. He stopped work on a cross-desert racing truck with 24 inches of suspension movement to talk on how he sees the job at which he has successfully avoided starving for nearly 30 years.

"I built my first special at 15, but I never thought of myself as a designer. I only say that now because I don't actually make the parts with my own hands. I can draw, weld, fabricate, lay up fibreglass. I've worked as a freelance for the Japanese, for Rick Galles and Dan Gurney, for Don Nichols who founded Shadow, and a lot of racers to keep the money flowing. The job and earnings are always erratic. I designed an up-and-down pedal cycle, and then an infinitely variable gear to earn the money to support my own racing. It earned me 60,000 dollars but finally the options were not taken up though I still hold the valid patents.

"I believe I'm the only American ever to have designed complete cars for both Nissan and Toyota. The secret project for Toyota in 1967 seemed to be some kind of exercise - very curious altogether. It just disappeared into the cellars after completion.

"There are no courses for race car designers. I think the only way to really learn this business is to build the parts with your own hands. If you haven't done this I question how you can design parts that can be made by other people.

"One fundamental is that no matter how good a vehicle is, if it is difficult to work on you will be beaten by one that can be adjusted more quickly. Better to work on it than dream about it. This is a very practical business and simplicity is an extremely high priority. But there is no cast-iron list of priorities, they will vary with the vehicle and what it has to do, and you have to get these right first, whether it be ground clearance, fitting a particular engine, downforce, whatever.

"Looking at the most recent project, the IMSA for Nissan; it had to be an update an an existing car, followed by a completely new one. I was given four months and a much altered three year old Lola T810 without budget or time for a new car. I made four initial decisions:

1. There was neither money nor time for a new rear suspension, it had to stay.
2. The tub needed to be much stiffer which meant a complete new one from scratch.
3. A complete new front suspension, both geometry and because accessibility was poor; it was difficult even to change coils and space was very limited.
4. Despite 3, I might have to use the original front uprights at least to begin with.

"Assuming you have taken care of fundamental stiffness and geometry, aerodynamics have to be vital. You need the

Trevor Harris: 35 years experience of racing car design. He was visited by the author at his Santa Ana base in his native USA.

highest downforce with the lowest drag that can be achieved. And you cannot combine a high downforce car with a flexible chassis. Downforce and stiffness go hand in hand, and rigidity includes suspension links, uprights or hub carriers and mounting points. For instance, I much prefer fabricated uprights to cast ones. Castings have too many problems in manufacture for my liking - wall thickness, internal voids and so on.

"Designers like to assume they have done a really good job and will not normally like to subject their product to actual test. But they must remember they can screw up and be willing to admit it and make changes.

"You cannot reduce the unwanted in a design to zero - you can only hope to minimise what is not good. You can draw the position of the Roll Centre in static geometry but the dynamic position is a different matter. The point about which the car rolls can be totally modified by altering the springs, or the weight transfer and the consequent loading on the tyres.

"Tyres are something of an unknown. A race tyre can have, say, a rate of 1500 inch/lbs. and rising, but you don't know how that rate will alter. I've asked for data. When Firestone agreed to make special tiny tyres for Don Nichols' Frisbee

Harris supervises construction of the brand new tub for the 1988 Nissan GTP car in the California workshop of ex-Lotus man Jim Chapman (far right) with fellow Englishman John Saunders-Hyde (centre).

Can Am car, I asked their top brass exactly those questions at the time. They said they had never been asked them before and never carried out any tests to find answers.

"I don't feel I have ever personally done a definitive step forward. It is technology that forces things forward. I keep asking myself 'what is the next technology'? Perhaps my perimeter spoiler - a projecting lip all round the bottom edge of the all-enveloping body was my biggest step at the time. It is appearing on road cars 20 years later, but it has been a bit of a trademark of mine.

"I recall one of the most satisfying things I've ever done was a front suspension package for Shadow that put everything into a tiny space. It was a private satisfaction combining looks with efficiency. If a thing looks bad I cannot do it. Parts for me are alive; they have a character to them. This business is more than engineering. The day a computer is able to do both a real neat looking part, and the whole job as well, I'll get out".

Tony Southgate is a freelance working from his village home in Northamptonshire. He has been designer or consultant to many major teams over the years, including Lola, BRM, Shadow, Arrows, Chevron and Osella. At the time of writing he was in a third year with Jaguar for their highly successful return to the World Sports-Prototype Championship.

A few years ago, at the height of Porsche's domination of the WSPC, Southgate was bold enough to observe publicly that he felt the 956/962 left a lot to be desired and should be beatable with a more up-to-date approach. In due course, when Jaguar re-entered the fray, he got his chance.

"The 962 had been the car to beat for some time. It was quite obvious the chassis side was very basic, fairly flimsy construction, which meant that the suspension side was not working as it should and the aerodynamics were very bitty. Stresses give the engine a hard time and crankcases start to break up. Porsche have the resources but are very slow to respond to racing needs. Their Indy Car was an example - I looked at it and it was a three year old car. They work like a big corporation and worry about their reputation. A small team does it now and cannot worry about that. The Jaguar was all about trying to do it right.

"When I left school I did an engineering apprenticeship as a design draughtsman in a contract office. You get everything there, allsorts. Then I went to work for Eric Broadley at Lola for five years. In some ways I thought I was better

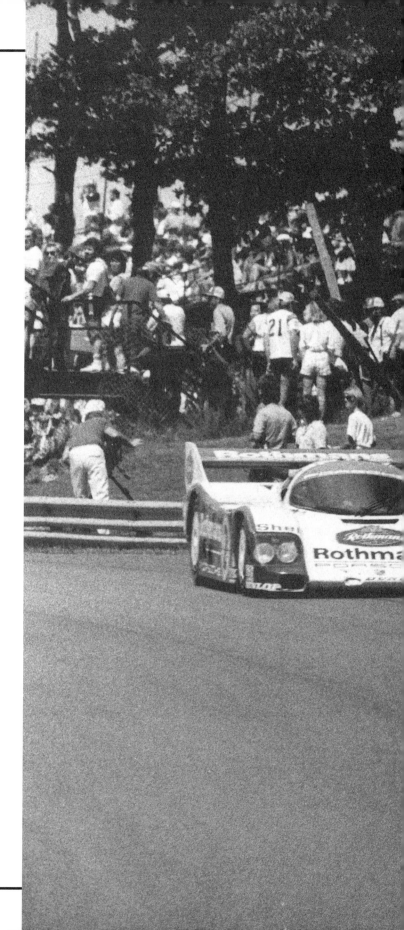

Jaguar leads Porsche at Mosport, '85. Southgate's superb chassis would often show a clean pair of heels to the cars from Stuttgart, previously virtually unbeatable in the Group C arena.

than Eric - he'd been a quantity surveyor and some of his early drawings were on the back of old quotes, while I knew about heat treatment and things.

"But he sent me down to a wind tunnel in London to put small models in it. The experts there had no idea, they couldn't talk car language and all racing cars looked like an E-Type which didn't work. My knowledge on spoilers and lips and things was all self taught and while I wasn't quite sure how or why they worked, they did.

"It was difficult in those days. Now you never plot a suspension - you just press a few buttons - but the first move still has to be by a human being. Electronic gadgets do the

Tony Southgate on the Silverstone pit wall (left) contemplating the start of the 1988 1000km. race (above) - a straight fight between Jaguar and Mercedes. Jaguar won.

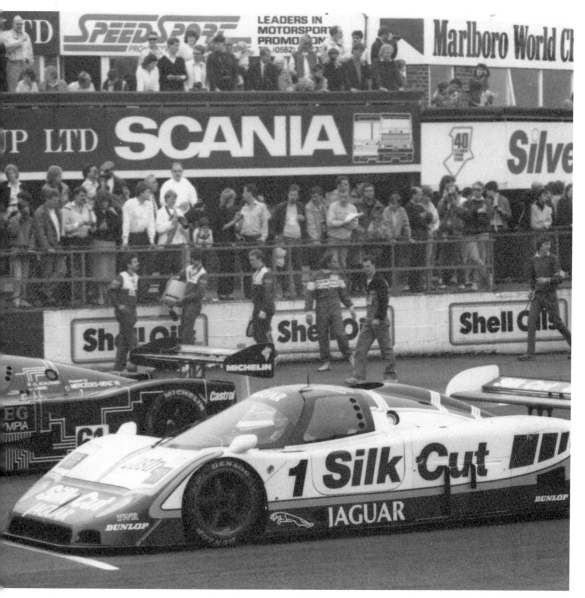

plot, but you still have to decide what you want and where your points are going to be. You must still decide that.

"I don't have a single reference book in my office. Well, just one I think, Costin and Phipps from a long time ago. Design is largely evolution. You rarely go completely mad and revolutionary. You might hear its happened, but everything has been done before in 1901 or so. The clever thing is to put it on a racing car and make it go out and win races.

"It's how I think. You look at everything you've done before. You look at other peoples' work. You feel you can improve and don't give any secrets away. We do still look at roll centre and geometry, but if I gave you positions or camber change details my opposition would think I was mental - or they wouldn't believe them.

"You are under severe pressure in all racing. I wouldn't want to be working at Ligier at the moment (the brand new Judd car had just failed to even qualify at Rio). If it all works you are the big hero but if it doesn't you have very few friends...

"The most interesting of current suspensions has to be the Williams. The Jaguar is almost antique compared to computer control. I tried to buy Lotus Active on behalf of TWR but they wanted a million pounds or something for the principles, let alone buying the hardware.

"The starting point of a design is not always the same. With the Jag I was told, 'do what you like, but use this V12'. You have to come to grips with that - you very rarely start with nothing.

"Suspension is less important at first, but much more so when the car is up and running. In the design stage it is low among my priorities, for ground effects and the engine size and shape influence the type. You certainly don't say, "I'll have pull rod, or push rod", but you have the general idea

of what you want - ideally it will be like this but you might have to compromise on it a lot.

"Aerodynamics come first, but again you have to be realistic. You might have to throw away some advantage because it is simply not practical, is inaccessible or too heavy. Too much work to do on a car in the time available will defeat you.

"At the end of the day it has to be a practical car. Above all you have to have reliability. You need durability to run 24 hours plus practice at full racing speeds. There is a lot of pushing and hitting each other in sports cars, always scratches and wheel marks on the sides when drivers come in. It is not usually deliberate but they are very close to each other so some things look pretty beefy in a sports car, and you design bodywork to be strong and not to have bits sticking out that can get knocked off.

"The Jag project has been satisfying. It is three years old now and still looks quite good. There have been changes en route but the suspension system in its day was quite interesting because of one thing and another".

What one thing and another? Southgate moves the conversation immediately to the 1982 Osella...

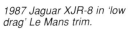

1987 Jaguar XJR-8 in 'low drag' Le Mans trim.

"Osella was a little team with no money then, but I did a front end with bellcranks and co-axial roll bar which made a very nice compact installation".

Any disasters? He affects to remember only one - and that by Lotus.

"That terrible all-adjustable 77. When they first put it on its wheels it collapsed onto the ground... The Jag has had only two structural failures in three and a half years. One was a wishbone, and personally I think it hit something, but I redesigned it anyway.

"When you are young you believe anything, and then experience seems to disprove the theories so often it makes you wonder what the hell it is makes it work at all. You put a proven suspension on one car and it's fine. You put it on another and it is hopeless. It is so easy to lose track. You have to keep a very open mind, stay flexible and change, if necessary, on the day. If it's wrong, you must bite the bullet and throw it away".

Gordon Murray took over the design "hot seat" at McLaren after John Barnard departed to Ferrari. He had never worked full-time professionally for anyone but Brabham, but his first McLaren stupefied the whole of Formula One by qualifying 3.5 seconds faster than any other car in its second race, a degree of superiority almost unique in motor racing.

The road began as a racing obsessed teenager in South Africa, building his own special, working in an engineering factory while doing a sandwich course in mechanical engineering at the local technical college. Barely 20, he sold the special - and everything else he owned - for the fare to Britain and a job in motor racing if he could find one.

"Designing used to be such a solitary thing - all think and talk to yourself, but I don't know if there is such as a racing car designer any more. I was the only one in the drawing office when I started at Brabham. Nowadays I hardly pick up a pencil and have a team of 16 people. It has moved on to being leader of a team.

"Most of Formula One is evolutionary. The apparently new nearly always happens because of some outside influence - new regulations, different engine, or perhaps the end of the road with no light at the end of the tunnel with the current car. You run out of flexibility with it, and you are very lucky to get three seasons out of a Formula One car.

"There are certain parameters you cannot alter; fuel capacity, size and weight of the driver, the wheels and tyres. If we

Gordon Murray and Nelson Piquet: a combination that won two World titles for Brabham using Cosworth and BMW engines. This shot was taken in '84, at Imola with the BMW-propelled BT53. Overleaf is pictured the rear suspension of the essentially similar BT54 of 1985.

lost Alain (Prost) it would mean a new car. It is tailored to him to half an inch everywhere.

"The first aim is to separate out the good and bad points of the previous car - get the drivers to be absolutely frank about what they liked or didn't like, its vices and its strengths. Then you have to try and eliminate the vices and keep the strong points. You have to sort out what you want to do to make it better. When you've added in a cooling package and a planned weight distribution you have very little elbow room.

"To alter the suspension is easy but if you find you have lost good turn in or something in the process, it becomes a very complex thing. Once you have made the decisions on the basics you go to the wind tunnel - let the aerodynamicist loose. You have to have a good aerodynamic package, what I would call the first level of importance.

"Suspension is still very relevant. You have to decide on the geometry you want and to do the layouts for it, but it does tend to get compromised more than it should because it is one of the few areas in which you can make alterations to some degree. Once you have settled the geometry, fitting it in is one of the last things in many ways.

"You need straight load paths, of course, with light weight and strength and all these can be quite difficult to achieve. There are a lot of very complicated suspension systems these days, but I prefer to keep it as simple as can be achieved. This is what you might call the second level of importance and the third level is all the minor stuff.

"Movement of the suspension has become of less consequence. It has been more and more constrained since 1983 (instigation of flat bottoms) since you have to run cars extremely low with little bump and little droop. This became as small as 1.5 inches in ground effect days, but it crept back up a little, to 2 inches or so at present.

Weight distribution is veering back to 40f/60r again, although it was about 45/55 in ground effect days with the driver much further forward.

"The biggest long term factor in a car is the engine. You need if at all possible to stay with the same one for a number of years. At Brabham I had to do everything again from scratch with three totally different engines and I'm doing it again with the Honda. You need a new everything and then to go out and try to win...

"Satisfying achievements? Well, I always hated those little tube brackets and frameworks hanging off things, and I

Teo Fabi in full flight in the Brabham BT53. Note the push rod front suspension.

moved to special or modified castings feeding suspension loads straight into the gearbox and the Cosworth DFV cylinder heads. I did bulkheads machined from solid rather than fabrications. We had a carbon fibre monocoque parts for the Alfa V12 in the late Seventies and I think the first carbon discs and pads. We really struggled with those - every kind of trouble but they were, and are, such a big help with unsprung weight and inertia loads. And they saved 30 lbs. on a full car set.

"I did a pull rod front suspension on the BT44, but that was actually three years old then. What happened was that soon after I got to England I discovered this magic formula - 750 Racing - incredibly cheap with very few restrictions. I went round the paddock at Silverstone with a camera and black and white film and decided that I had a chance of winning if I built a monocoque, very light with the lowest possible centre of gravity. Given these two and comparable power you will win, although being six foot four inches didn't help.

"To get the lightest possible wishbones, I had to get rid of the bending loads in the bottom front from mounting the coil and damper on it, which was pretty general in 1970. Some of those bottom wishbones would have held the world up, and with restricted room I came up with a linkage with a bellcrank at the bottom so I could lay the suspension units down. I made the suspension and began the monocoque but I was working such long hours trying to get somewhere it was never finished. But when I was doing the BT44, I decided to lift the whole front end from my 750 design. It saved me a month of working and thinking, and had quite an impact and everyone uses pull or push rods now.

Murray reflects on the ill-fated, lowline BT55 with its heavily canted BMW engine.

"Well, the new McLaren (the 1988 MP3) is the same height and has exactly the same driving position as the '55. There were four reasons why it did not win.

"With hindsight, I was much too ambitious in how much we lowered it. The rather tall BMW had to lie down so far it produced a heavily offset crank needing a special gearbox and drivetrain, and what I did wrong was to try to do it in the time available.

"Secondly, the engine never worked properly in the lay down position. The exhaust and turbo system was a night-

Senna in the low line 1988 Honda-McLaren, the car that ran from its rivals and hid.

mare and it had incurable oil surge and drain problems in corners. One way it was OK, but not the other.

"The weight distribution gave dynamic c. of g. movements that messed up the traction.

"And then Bernie (Ecclestone, owner of the team) who is totally non-technical and had always left that side completely to me, started to get involved in the technical side. We had had 16 years with never a cross word until then, and things were changing with his deeper and deeper involvement in FOCA.

"Then McLaren made approaches to me and I just felt it was the end of the road at Brabham. It was really the only place I could go for a step up and a totally new challenge".

The results of that new challenge took 16 months to arrive on the grid and left opposition timekeepers staring at stopwatches in stupefied disbelief, so great was the initial superiority in the hands of two of the better drivers of all time - Prost and Senna. Would he - can he - say why?

"Well, it's a very simple car, very low, with a good aerodynamic package. Chapman laid the driver right back - it's not a new idea, and drivers will never sit right up again. It has a lot of good flow to the rear wing and low frontal area. It is a simple basic design particularly at the front where everyone has got very complicated on suspension. We're quite pleased with how it has gone".

The Amateur At Work

...a long-standing tradition

7

The author at work in his '84 Terrapin at Harewood, en route to his personal best ever time at the British hillclimb venue (43.25 seconds).

By no means all readers will be necessarily enthralled with the idea of showing the rest of the world just how it should be done. But for those who feel that more exact details of the approach, some simple maths, finalising geometry and coils and roll bars and so on, have been a bit sparse up to now, there follows one man's approach - mine.

To be more exact and more honest, a distillation of much I have heard, read, discussed, theorised upon and taken to practical experiment in a number of cars, together with friends of like mind and obsession. In case you should find the following in any way unsatisfactory, unsuitable to your needs, or dubious from start to finish, blame me rather than the friends. Risking such verdicts, we will consider how the general design of a racing car, and the specific aspects of a suspension that has a decent chance of working without a fundamental redesign may be tackled by somebody outside professional circles.

Bear in mind that just about everyone of current fame and success was "outside professional circles" when first starting. Colin Chapman was 'moonlighting' in a North London lock up building his 750 Austin Seven before he was a world figure. Eric Broadley's Lola was a side-valved Ford club racer before it was an Indycar or a Grand Prix car. John Barnard designed model boats long years previous to McLaren and Ferrari. Adrian Reynard was constructing his own special and addressing local motor club meetings on the finer points of the art on his way up the ladder. Gordon Murray built not only his own racing car but much of its Ford-based engine including pistons before ever leaving South Africa for unknown Britain.

None of them seem to have followed a formal route into motor racing design, even if there has ever been one. Some have a high level of technological education or experience (though aimed at other targets) and some do not. As the Greek shipping tycoon Aristotle Onassis is said to have observed: "The only rule is that there are no rules", and for a small select group this seems to be true as they take unorthodox ways to the top with talents somewhat hard to define.

They utilise those talents in a sport with high technological content, in which there is undoubtedly a 'Great Divide' between those with virtually unlimited money and resources, and those who have less, a lot less or are very pushed indeed. In reality all share almost every difficulty with each other, but will have to solve those difficulties in different ways, with a different sequence to their priorities.

For instance: it is difficult to refute the point of view that all suspension design must begin with the tyre, while spring frequencies, geometry, weight transfer and a dozen other parameters are tailored to the rate and characteristics of the carcase and compound. The flaws in the practical application of this standpoint are two-fold. Tyres are still a very difficult manufactured object in which to forecast precisely how they will perform in a variety of situations. And should such forecasts be available - and they verge on the impossible to extract from any tyre firm - the amateur cannot influence or alter them in any way.

In truth he can, just a little, by altering pressures (and hence the rate) and fitting them onto varying widths of rim (which will alter the carcase stability and performance under cornering forces). And this is barely less than the professionals can manage with a control tyre available to any entrant.

"Beyond here lie dragons" the old mapmakers inscribed when reliable information dried up completely. Such ignorance does not obliterate the need to give the tyre contact patch, the single most important thing on a racing car, the very best chance to perform to its maximum. This might be loosely defined as keeping it flat on the road, distorting it as little as practicable, not grossly over - or under - loading it at front or rear, and keeping it as near a proper running temperature as climate or speeds allow.

It may come as some surprise to know the precise detailing of the chassis/tub will not be near the top of our list. Only its stiffness is vital. Its function is that of a large, complex bracket, with the sole job in life of locating accurately and rigidly in space the various components ranging from suspension pivots to the driver's backside. It must fit them, not the other way round.

We have already considered to some degree how important are the current regulations in force and how they have to come first. A never ending war, Rulemakers versus The Rest, ensures that the fabric of those rules is forever bending, creaking and sometimes giving way completely under the unrelenting pressures of the determined, the devious and the frankly dubious, fuelled by immense sums of money at the top levels of the sport.

"Reading the regs." is step one. It is no use to arrive in the first scrutineering bay with a world beater that is just slightly the wrong size. Sounds very basic? It is, but it has still happened painfully publicly to some of the most experienced; McLaren for one, concerning a little matter of overall width, and Osella losing to Italian scrutineers in a "new car or modified one" argument . Other requirements can include safety standards, materials, wheel travel, wheelbase and track, tyre and rim sizes, body dimensions, overhang sideways, forward and back, cockpit size and access - the list seems never ending.

Once the small print has been digested, the first move is to do side and plan views to scale of the items that must be part of the finished car and permit no variation. These will include the human being that will drive it, engine/gearbox unit, fuel tank whether 2 or 42 gallons, oil tank if dry sumped, the steering wheel and gear lever, and the line on which the pedals and thus the driver's feet will lie.

We could go into a lot of detail on these aspects, and the various and graceful solutions that have been found to them over the years, but they will have to give way to the prime objective here - suspension.

Once you are embarked, the sequence often appears to work backwards. Firstly one decides what is wanted and then one moves on to try and achieve it.

The Priority List:

1. Regulations.
2. Tyres.
3. Wheels.
4. Hubs and uprights.
5. Geometry.
6. Roll centre.
7. Instantaneous roll centre/ swing axle length.
8. Springs.
9. Dampers.
10. Anti roll bars.
11. Steering.

Regulations

The importance of these has already been discussed. For UK competitors, the main source will be the RACMSA's "Blue Book" which comes free with each competition licence.

Tyres

The enormous availability and variety of the 13 inch diameter tyre, whether new or "slightly scuffed" makes it highly likely to be the first choice. Any larger diameter is usually employed only because vehicle size or power forces the option. The smaller 12 inch is a rare bird, and the desirable (from a weight and inertia point of view) 10 inch Mini size suffers from a marked lack of choice in width, construction and tread compounds.

Wheels

These will be totally dictated by tyre size and the type of centre fixing or stud pattern of the hub flange. Do not invest any of your funding into wheels, however attractive and low priced, until you know exactly how and to what they will be attached. It is far easier to obtain a wheel with the centre you require than to alter a hub and flange to suit the wrong wheel.

Hubs and uprights.

Although technically two items, together with their bearings, spacers and seals, they are so closely inter-related as to be a single component. In one swoop, it dictates wheels, offsets (or insets, if you prefer), method of attachment, and the vital positions of the upper and lower outboard suspension pick ups. The professional would have these made to his own dimensions, whether cast or fabricated, but the amateur can often alter pick ups, especially up or down, by designing his own bushes, spacer plates or inserted pins to modify the upright. This is a valid example of first deciding what you need, and only then setting about achieving it.

Happily it may not be necessary because, as we shall see fairly soon, the aims of the final suspension geometry can very often be achieved utilising outboard points already chosen by somebody else for a different situation.

Geometry

Any decision on springs, anti roll bars, weight transfer or wheel frequencies cannot be made until the lengths, angles and pick up positions of the wishbones have been finalised. But the basic injunction to "stay low" where centre of gravity and roll centre are concerned is a vital one to keep to the fore.

We are now at the heart of things, and that heart - in my view at least - is The Roll Centre.

You have to have at least one firm base on which to begin creating your suspension design, and nothing I have been involved with over some years has shaken my conviction that the best, and possibly the only, reliable starting point is the Roll Centre. You have to cling on to something.

Where the roll centre is located statically in various designs of suspension can most clearly be seen in drawings rather than attempting any explanation in words. What it is, at least theoretically, is the point in space about which the vehicle will rotate when it leans over in a corner. As this point will dictate how the chassis suspension pick up points move, and hence what the wheel and tyre will then do, the importance of controlling its position in space, should this be possible, will be clear.

The trouble with all theoretical suspension concepts is that they alter once real life cornering and other forces come into play, because the static data on which they are based alters. The Dynamic Roll Centre (as opposed to the static one) can and does move up, down, and sideways. How far and which way are two of several questions not easy to answer.

Roll being itself a function of another moveable and equally invisible point, the Centre of Gravity (which moves forward under braking, backwards under acceleration and sideways in a corner), it can be seen how the variations and uncertainties are rapidly multiplying. Leverages alter, the car's attitude alters, weight transfer from inner to outer wheels alters, and at the end of the line, the tyre contact patches start distorting under a complex and varying series of loads.

Such uncertainties do not invalidate careful pre-planning and design, otherwise one car, however laid out or badly unbalanced would work as well as any other. Clearly this is not the case, so how to make a start?

Currently there are four options:

i) Copy exactly, through friendship or purchase, a successful design already running. The obvious hurdle in this is that every point in it that moves must be reproduced precisely in space, and a suitable identical upright may not exist. And once your copy begins to diverge from the original potential roadholding shortcomings creep in. You must anyway make your own analysis of it or any future modifications will be fumbling in the dark.

ii) Draw your proposed layout, then re-draw and re-draw with gradual movements of wheel and chassis in bump, roll and droop. You will soon be into scores and then hundreds of drawings while researching variations of variations. Barely practical even for the drawing office of a major manufacturer.

iii) Use a computer to vary a mathematical model of your brainchild. The prime virtue of the computer - its ability to do a million or 100 million repetitive calculations at high speed in search of a solution - is perfectly suited to the task. What is much more difficult is creating a suitable programme (a set of instructions which it can follow), though at least one is already on the commercial market, together with an analysis and design service.

The major teams and big manufacturers have been into computer technology for quite some time but apparently still without producing the perfect answer. One reason for this may well be deciding the questions that need to be asked in the first place, as well as interpreting the answers. The human brain is still paramount in interpolating what the computer will spew out.

iv) The String Computer. Born of desperate necessity when Richard Blackmore and I were designing the first Terrapin (Mini rear-engined, spaceframe chassisied single seater) at a time when computers were room sized and cost a million pounds or so. The approach was to make a working model of an unequal length wishbone suspension to scale and to give it freedom to move not only the wheel and upright but also to rotate the chassis and wishbones about a roll centre. Finally the string supplied a way of indicating in small increments what the roll centre might be doing. It was easy and cheap to make, and proved such a good basic, if apparently crude tool that later cross-checks when computers had made the downward mega-leap into every high street electrical shop showed that the results it gave correlated quite closely with the electronic versions. It was not able by its construction to work to much closer than 0.125 inch, while a computer operates to a "thou" or less if you ask it.

This is not a really major handicap as the critical thing is achieving the right objectives within reasonable limits rather than getting the wrong ones with total accuracy. Its worst shortcoming is that very long Swing Axle Lengths, when the wishbones approach nearer and nearer to parallel, make manipulation of the string impossible. However, half scale and a friend operating at the far end of a long room will overcome all but the most extreme situations. Details of its costruction and use are given in Appendix 1.

First experiments indicate that roll centres do indeed move sideways under some circumstances, as well as up and down. This can be shown by using the computer to plot first an outer wheel, then an inner wheel (left roll, then right roll). Unless you have hit the jackpot first go, and the roll centre stays at an unaltered height it will normally rise for one wheel and fall for the other. Clearly it cannot be in two places at once, and it has in fact moved sideways to the intersection of the two lines joining the instantaneous roll centres to the tyre contact patches. Careful experimentation can reduce this to almost negligible proportions.

While roll centre and geometry in general have been publicly rubbished as unimportant by some designers, it is clear from analysing various competition cars that the close control of the roll centre (sometimes within .015 - .020 over the total wheel travel) is beyond luck and has demanded a good deal of private attention.

We can now get down to more detail, attempting to quantify and define a few aims, and then consider how to achieve them - should they be achievable.

Roll Centre

The roll centre lies in the bracket between an inch below ground to (at worst) some 12 inches above, in the case of the centre of a solid axle. All racing cars are probably now located within one inch below to two inches above ground. Low centres give less weight transfer to the outer wheel, smaller or nil jacking effect but high potential roll angles. Suitable and variable anti roll bars must handle this. Front and rear centres are conventionally at different heights to give a tilted Roll Axis with the lower centre at the lowest and/or lightest end of the vehicle but this is by no means universal.

Instantaneous Roll Centre/ Swing Axle Length

These are another couple of invisible variables in less than precise ways. IRC is the intersection point of lines drawn along the wishbones, and SAL is the distance from this point back to the wheel.

Short SAL (20 - 40 inches) gives very good roll centre location, keeps the outer wheel vertical in corners, but going badly to positive camber in droop and negative in bump (acceleration squat and braking).

Long SAL (70 - 180 inches) provides lower roll centres but less control over their sideways movement, minimal scrub (track variation), poor outer wheel control going into positive camber, but only small camber change in bump/droop.

Medium SAL (40 - 70 inches) is the transition area between long and short with, as you might expect, a bit of this and a bit of that.

Ultra-long SAL (near parallel: one example had 14,000 inches) provides excellent vertical control of very low roll centres but possible enormous sideways movement, wheel angles virtually unaltered in bump/droop but very poor control of wheels in roll, with near equivalency to body roll angle.

It will be evident from all this that, as in life, you cannot have everything. Roll effects, wheel angle, scrub and roll centre location have to be balanced against each other and different situations (circuit, hillclimb; free or restricted tyre width; tolerable roll angle or ground clearance) may demand different priorities.

Having discussed an approach that costs literally nothing, the use of a computer is so much faster it permits of vastly more experiment in the limited time any of us have available. A company commercially specialising in the field may be worth an investment but while this will provide an analysis together with a set of suggestions for new or modified settings/ dimensions it may not help you depart from, modify or progress from those baselines. It is the electronic equivalent of having the car set up by an expert. He supplies the results, but no secrets.

Doing it on your own home computer demands a programme of some complexity, but certainly not beyond a reasonable maths student with tenacity. I know at least three who have done it in various forms so there have to be many others.

To grossly oversimplify, you have to reduce the suspension dimensions to a number of triangles that will vary in a sequential as well as interrelated way in the length of their sides and their angles. Not all small computers can cope with the demands, so research is needed, but having seen and used the David Gould-written programme (Gould as in Chapter Eight) its attractions are considerable.

But even with such a facility, comprehension of the principles and specific aims are still needed as you have to feed data in before you get answers out.

Remembering that we began with the tyre, the String Computer is literally as well as metaphorically a "wooden wheel" model. It cannot really insert deflection under load of the tyre carcase, although a rough attempt can be made by mis-setting the bottom of the wheel on the "road" to reproduce your estimate of how much the carcase has deflected. As this has to be the most-difficult -to-quantify variable by a considerable margin, you will have to decide whether to do totally without it, or take the gamble of an attempted inclusion. Either way, never forget that the wider the tyre, the less happy and efficient it will be as it leans away from the vertical. Keeping the tread area flat on the ground so far as humanly possible is of the highest priority.

Springs

Taken for sake of simplicity to be coils, and another example where we work backwards to find what is required. The key to the decision is a formula that combines the coil rate, the leverage on it, and the sprung weight that will rest on it. These permit a direct comparison of "softness" or ride quality between a Formula One car, a road saloon car and a loaded 30 ton tanker if you should so wish. It is known as the natural frequency of the suspension, quoted either in Cycles per minute (CPM) or per second (Hertz or Hz).

Before coming to the formulae themselves, we need to have an idea of what is in or out of the ballpark. Although it has been said that an ideal frequency is that of a man walking normally - some 120 CPM - riding in a wheeled vehicle turns out to be a different matter, and experience of millions of road and sports cars has produced a reasonable guide to the practical frequencies. These lie in the 60 - 80 CPM bracket for comfortable road cars, 80 - 100 for firmer

Suspension frequency examples and calculation method.

Data	1 Wheel frequency (CPM) F	2 Sprung weight (net corner wt. in lbs) SW	3 Susp. leverage SL	4 Susp. leverage squared SL²	5 Effective Coil Rate lbs/ins ECR	6 Coil crush (inches Static) Crush	7 Wheel Rate (lbs/ins) WR	8 Static Deflection (inches) SD	9 Coil Rate (lbs/in) CR	Remarks CR is actual spring fitted to vehicle
How obtained	Designer's choice or $187.8\sqrt{\dfrac{WR}{SW}}$	Gross corner wt. less unsprung wt.	Designer's Calc. choice or Measure		Calc. $\dfrac{CR}{SL}$	Calc. $\dfrac{SWXSL}{CR}$	Calc. SW or $\dfrac{ECR}{CR}$ $\dfrac{CR}{SL^2}$	Calc. $\dfrac{SW}{WR}$	Designer's choice or WRXSL² or ECRX SL	
Gould Terrapin 1600 cc (1980 to 1983) Data: Gross Wt. with drive 1060 lbs. Front: 384 lbs. Rear: 676 lbs.	Front: 102	138	2.0:1	4.0:1	80	1.31	40	3.45	160	First experiment
	Front: 107.3	138	2.0:1	4.0:1	90	1.17	45	3.1	180	Better
	Front: 113	138	2.0:1	4.0:1	100	1.05	50	2.76	200	Better
	Front: 120	138	2.0:1	4.0:1	112.5	0.93	56.5	2.44	225	Less improvement
	Front: 126.5	138	2.0:1	4.0:1	125	0.84	62.5	2.21	250	"Over the edge" but retained
	Front: 132.7	138	2.0:1	4.0:1	137.5	0.76	68.75	2.00	275	Too hard
	Front: 96.3	238	2.0:1	4.0:1	125	1.64	62.5	3.81	250	Ground effect of 0.55G (400 lb split equally to each wheel)
Sprung Wts. $\dfrac{384}{2}-54=138$ lbs. Front $\dfrac{676}{.2}-58=280$ lbs. Rear	Rear: 113.5	280	1.565:1	2.45:1	159.7	1.59	102	2.74	250	First experiment
	Rear: 120	280	1.565:1	2.45:1	178.9	1.42	114	2.46	280	Better
	Rear: 124.3	280	1.565:1	2.45:1	191.7	1.33	122.5	2.28	300	Better
	Rear: 129.4	280	1.565:1	2.45:1	207.7	1.23	133	2.10	325	Final choice
	Rear: 111.2	380	1.565:1	2.45:1	207.7	1.58	133	2.86	325	Ground effect of 0.550 (400 lb split equally to each wheel)
	Rear: 134.3	280	1.565:1	2.45:1	236.6	2.14	143	1.96	350	Future plan
LT25: F5000 (Len Terry design)	Front: 118	230	1.87:1	3.49:1	167.9	1.37	89	2.58	314	From "Racing Car Design and Development
	Rear: 125	440	1.36:1	1.85:1	269.8	1.63	195	2.26	367	
March 763 (1976 F3)	Front: 104	190	1.75:1	3.06:1	102.8	1.85	58.8	3.23	180	Pre-ground effect circuit car
	Rear: 119.5	310	1.27:1	1.61:1	159	1.95	125.5	2.47	202	
Typical F1 ground effect car showing results of varying downforce (pre-'83)	Front: 410	315	2.0:1	4.0:1	3000	0.1	1500	0.21	6000	Note on weight calcs: Formula Minimum 580 kg = 1276 lb
	Rear: 504	385	1.2:1	1.44:1	3.333	0.16	2.777	0.14	4000	Driver = 164 lb ½ fuel = 160 lb 1600 lb
		very low speed								
	Front: 290	630	2.0:1	4.0:1	3000	0.2	1500	0.42	6000	45%F = 720 lb
	Rear: 357	770	1.2:1	1.44:1	3.333	0.23	2.777	0.28	4000	55R = 880 lb Est sprung wt. per corner:
		Medium speed								F: 315 lbs R: 385 lbs
	Front: 237	945	2.0:1	4.0:1	3000	0.31	1500	0.63	6000	
	Rear: 291	1155	1.2:1	1.44:1	3.333	0.35	2.777	0.42	4000	
		High speed								
Rally Sunbeam 1600 (5 link rear axle and MacPherson Strut front)	Front: 78	495	1:1	1:1	85	5.8	85	5.8	85	Standard
	Rear: 95	310	1.24:1	1.54:1	97	3.2	80	3.875	120	Standard
	Front: 102	495	1:1	1:1	145	3.4	145	3.4	145	First experiment loose
	Rear: 133	310	1.24:1	1.54:1	194	1.6	156	1.98	240	Final choice for loose
	Front: 118	495	1:1	1:1	195	2.54	195	2.54	195	
	Rear: 120	310	1.24:1	1.54:1	157	1.97	127	2.44	195	Final choice for tarmac
	Front: 128	495	1:1	1:1	230	2.15	230	2.15	2.30	
	Rear: 133	310	1.24:1	1.54:1	194	1.60	156	1.98	240	Tarmac experiment skewed roll onto front with bad U/steer
	Front: 118	495	1:1	1:1	195	2.54	195	2.54	195	
	Rear: 133	310	1.24:1	1.54:1	194	1.60	156	1.98	240	
	Front: 146	495	1:1	1:1	300	1.65	300,	1.65	300	Future tarmac "possible" for even less roll
	Rear: 161	310	1.24:1	1.54:1	282	1.75	227	1.36	350	

Note: Calculations *from* frequency required:

$$WR = \frac{Freq.^2 \times SW}{187.8} \qquad CR = WR \times SL^2 \text{ (then apply inclination correction if necessary (see page 200).}$$

and more sporting machinery, 100 - 125 for racing cars without wings or ground effect.

Beyond this, downforce which effectively increases the sprung weight and tiny ground clearances will mean that ever higher frequencies - or ever smaller movements of the car on its suspension - will be essential, however hard the ride, with the tyre taking over more and more of the spring's job. Figures of 160 - 200 CPM are nearer current trends, and at the peak of the ground effect era, cars left the grid at up to 500 CPM. Even when 3G and 4G downforce had pressed its iron hand down onto the cars, the wheel frequencies still lay between 200 and 300 which gave drivers a brutally harsh environment in which to work as well as an imperative need for good track surfaces.

A reasonable starting point is suggested as 110 CPM for a circuit car, plus or minus 15, and road, though not race, experience has shown that the front frequency needs to be about 10% lower than the rear. This is to avoid pitch, a nose up/nose down oscillation caused by the front wheels rising over a bump first, followed shortly afterwards by the rears. Once started, it is at best unpleasant and at worst is capable of sending a yumping rally car into a complete somersault.

However, practical experience on the track shows that on good surfaces with high frequency suspensions this "rule" is no longer necessarily valid, and front frequencies may well be higher than the rear when a search for better balance is going on. It is as well to remember that the deeper you go into the whole business, the less valid seem to be so many hitherto firm and reliable "rules". Do not feel that you have to abide by them, including any in these all-too- human pages.

There are also effectively three rates to any spring fitted to most vehicles. First is the Coil Rate, or the amount it compresses under a given load (in lbs./in. or N./mm.) usually etched or painted on it by the manufacturer. Second is the Fitted Rate, or how strong the spring appears to be on the car, taking into account the leverage on it exerted by the suspension linkage. An inboard mounted coil with a high leverage on it will be crushed more (and thus appear softer, or weaker) than a similar coil under similar load fitted to a MacPherson strut which exerts direct weight but no leverage, when Coil Rate and Fitted Rate will be the same.

The third rate is Wheel Rate, or how strong the spring appears to be to the wheel bouncing up and down at the end of its links and the calculation involves squaring the lever-

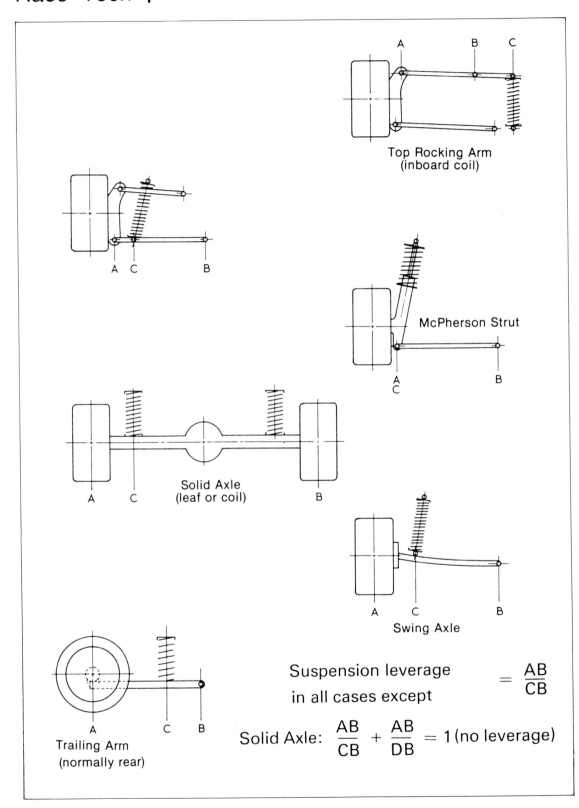

Top Rocking Arm
(inboard coil)

McPherson Strut

Solid Axle
(leaf or coil)

Swing Axle

Trailing Arm
(normally rear)

Suspension leverage in all cases except $= \dfrac{AB}{CB}$

Solid Axle: $\dfrac{AB}{CB} + \dfrac{AB}{DB} = 1$ (no leverage)

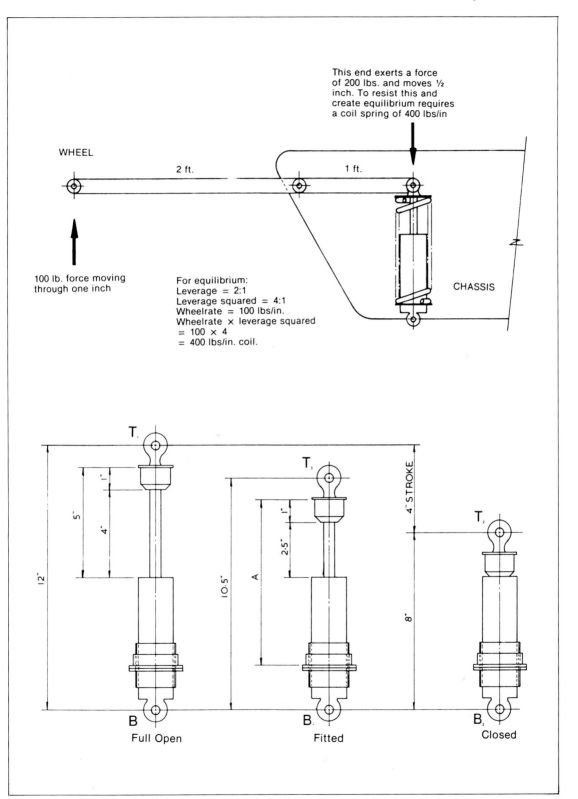

This end exerts a force of 200 lbs. and moves ½ inch. To resist this and create equilibrium requires a coil spring of 400 lbs/in

WHEEL

2 ft.   1 ft.

CHASSIS

100 lb. force moving through one inch

For equilibrium:
Leverage = 2:1
Leverage squared = 4:1
Wheelrate = 100 lbs/in.
Wheelrate × leverage squared
= 100 × 4
= 400 lbs/in. coil.

T₁   T₃   T₂

4" STROKE

12"   10.5"   8"

5"   2.5"
4"   1"
1"   A

B₁   B₃   B₂
Full Open   Fitted   Closed

age. For those readers possessing modest mathematical talents, the reason for this is illustrated, together with a number of examples of data for differing cars and the sequence for any calculations of your own.

The four formulae you will need are:

$$\text{Wheel Frequency CPM} = 187.8 \sqrt{\frac{\text{Wheel Rate lbs/in}}{\text{Sprung Weight lbs}}}$$

$$\frac{\text{Fitted Rate lbs/in}}{} = \frac{\text{Coil Rate lbs/in}}{\text{Susp. leverage}}$$

$$\frac{\text{Wheel Rate lbs/in}}{} = \frac{\text{Coil Rate lbs/in}}{\text{Susp. leverage}^2}$$

$$\text{or} \quad \left(\frac{\text{Wheel Frequ.}}{187.8}\right)^2 \times \text{Sprung Wt. lbs}$$

$$\text{Coil Rate} = \text{Wheel Rate} \times \text{Susp. Leverage}^2$$

These will allow you to go forwards or backwards depending what information you already have or need to find out.

A final point is that having decided on the rate of coil needed to do the job, a spring maker can produce the same thing in differing physical sizes by altering the wire diameter and number of coils, a great help if you are trying to get a particular spring into limited space.

Dampers.

The precise relationship between a damper, the coil surrounding it and the rest of the car is an extremely subtle and sensitive one, even in this day and age often being fine tuned by testing and "seat of the pants" feel once the car is running. Lotus for one earn substantial sums of money providing exactly this expertise to major manufacturers but as in so many areas, one needs at least a basic approach so that completely impossible units are avoided.

So long as leverages are the same (ie. a concentric coil/damper unit) the damper sees the coil - and deals with its attempts to oscillate - in terms of the actual rate or strength of that coil, ignoring inclinations, wheel rate, etc. The bump resistance of a damper is (almost) always less than the

Map of typical internal valving for the deservedly well known double-adjustable Koni damper. There are at least eight different sets of valves available tailored to coil springs ranging from 150 in./lbs. to 300 in./lbs. Single adjust patterns usually have a fixed bump resistance with any variations on rebound.

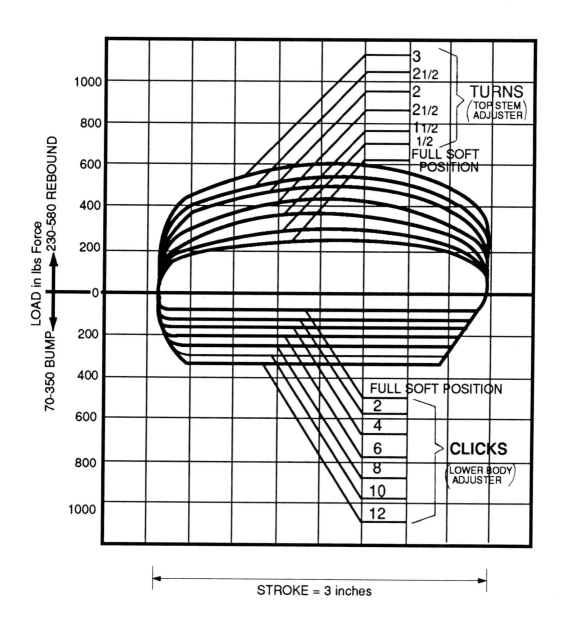

rebound - by a ratio of about 3 - 1 on an average road car, a relationship that has been distilled over many long years in the motor industry.

Racing brings the need for much tighter control. Gentle damping of a soft road coil demands considerable movement during which the forces have time to decay. The 10 inches total on a saloon or rally car may only be 2 inches on a circuit vehicle, with instantaneous loads from bumps or "kerbing" many many times higher. Comfort is a non-starter compared to grip and this sacrifice has brought the racing figure down to 2 or 1.5:1. As both bump and rebound can be made stronger while keeping the same proportional relationship both spring rates and varying car weights will alter the value of "strength".

So how are dampers quantified or calibrated? Usually in "force needed to open or compress it at a certain speed", ie. "150 rebound" could mean the unit requires a pull of 150 lbs. to move the piston out at 1 ft. per second, and any such figures are subject to a standardised temperature/oil viscosity specification. This is needed because the damper resistance is obtained by forcing the oil inside through tiny holes with very accurately made and sized valves. Oil viscosity is critical and the primary reason why dampers need to be protected from external heat and cooled as well, when it is borne in mind that real overwork will burn the paint off a damper body in minutes.

While knowledge of the precise units is obviously helpful, it may not be vital. Seeing 160/40 stamped on a casing will tell you that it is a 4:1 rebound/bump ratio, rather than 160/80 or 2:1.

When working, the damper allows the coil to do most of the work in absorbing the upward movement of the wheel whether as a result of a pothole, slight bump, or vehicle roll. Given a free hand, the spring would then use its stored energy to expand again, overstretch, contract and so on, in a series of diminishing or "decaying" oscillations - clearly the last thing that is wanted. This is where the strong rebound resistance of the damper comes in to prevent the spring getting going.

It will be seen that the power of the damper must be related in strength to the coil in some way. A 6000 lbs./in. coil will need a vastly stronger and differently valved unit to that suitable for a 100 lbs./coil. It would totally over-ride the weaker coil and stop it working as a spring at all.

Without setting up as a damper design consultant, it is

enough to know that the damper rebound/bump figures need to be "appropriate" to the coil. That is enough to indicate (if you have or can seek out the bump/rebound figures, not necessarily easy or even possible) whether you have the dampers that are in the ballpark or wildly unsuitable for the job, and the manufacturer of the damper must know this. All you have to do is ask, and hope he will be helpful. As a rough and ready guide, once you are ready to test:

Too much bump - very hard ride, sideways hop in corners.

Too much rebound - car jacks itself downwards, because spring is too weak to expand again after a bump.

Too little bump - grounding, excessive squat or nose dive, lurch onto front or rear corner.

Too little rebound - car bounces or wallows, lurch into corners.

A really massive mismatch is usually caused by big changes in coil rates (relatively cheap) without changing the dampers (much more expensive) and any competitions department would normally advise new damper figures for changes in coil rate, for instance, between tarmac and forest stage settings on a rally car.

It can be seen why double adjustable dampers, such as the deservedly famed Koni and the newest generation Spax are both expensive and vital for the finest of suspension tuning. Yet even these cannot cope outside a certain bracket without fundamental internal alteration. Koni has a range of at least eight basic internal factory settings, for example, for a series of spring rate groupings, which the sensitive external adjusters then further modify, and Spax will do similar modifications to their competition units.

Anti roll bars

Although there have been several successful, if complicated attempts to prevent a car rolling at all in a corner, or even to make it roll inwards like a banking aircraft, they are not in current competitive use, while roll is still with us, even in "active" suspension vehicles.

The initial and sometimes main resistance to roll comes from the the springs but there is a limit even on a racing car to which the springs can be made stronger and stronger simply to resist roll. They may also be resisting more at one end of the car than the other leading to a condition of "skewed roll" in which the car is visibly down on an outer front or rear wheel - a far from uncommon sight in races for saloons or older sports cars.

Bars appeared on the scene fairly early on, as a piece of non-adjustable bent steel rod, sometimes doing duty as an actual suspension link, and we have already had quite a detailed look at what they do and how in Chapter 2. It is now appropriate to try and quantify their power and plan how the bar can be used in a forecastable manner to strive for perfect balance for at least part of the time.

A truly sensitive and adjustable bar did not properly arrive until inboard suspension made a whole new design approach possible. Once there was a convenient, strong and geometrically pure point at the inboard end of a top rocking arm from which to twist a suitable bar, they became shorter and lighter, strong, needle-roller mounted for efficiency, and finely adjustable. Blades instead of bent ends also permitted remote alterations that allowed the driver a piece of the action in mid-race.

As we embark on design and installation of our bars, one aspect that may at first be difficult to get clear in the mind (it was in my case) is the exact strength of a given bar and precisely how you compare it to the coils. It is a matter which is complicated by bars having effectively two rates, one normally quoted in a pure engineering context and the other one that will relate it directly to the car's suspension.

The first is its Angular Rate in lbs./in./degree, or in radians. Without wishing to insult the mathematicians, a radian is actually 57.29578 degrees, or half a circle (180 degrees) divided by Pi (3.142). We will not go into why this figure may be more convenient in an academic situation but it is certainly far too large a deflection to work happily on a racing car and the degree is used from hereon.

To begin to correlate bar and coils, we have first to know or calculate its Angular Rate and the load in lbs./in. needed to twist it one degree along its length. We immediately discover that one degree can mean any linear distance depending on how far from the bar axis we are measuring, ie. how long is the lever arm? If our lever arm (the bent bit or blade at the end of the bar) is, say, four inches long, the tip will move a certain distance for one degree. Double the lever arm to eight inches and you double the distance moved by its tip, with the same load in lbs./in. - actually with half the force in lbs, over double the distance.

So we have a variable Linear Rate, dependant solely on

the length of the lever arm, while the Angular Rate stays constant. The car's interpretation of being able to move the lever arm twice as far with half the effort is, needless to say, that the bar has become very much weaker or softer.

But how much in terms of the coils? And what was it in the first place?

Once again we shall have to work backwards by first finding the roll moment of the whole car. We then assess how much the springs contribute to roll stiffness (remembering they have been chosen only in terms of wheel frequency and available suspension movement). From these two figures it will be possible to decide what further roll stiffness is required to limit roll with the target of around 2.5 degrees for a saloon and 1.5 degrees in a single seater at 1G cornering force as a maximum and preferably less.

These are somewhat arbitrary figures based partly on weights and leverages exerted within a typical saloon or single seater, and partly on the demands of certain geometries with which any increase in this amount of roll will produce wheel angles that are unacceptable.

But this is getting ahead of ourselves. We must forget, temporarily, any calculations to do with the bars and decide how and where they may best be fitted. Criteria are that they dodge the driver's legs, gearbox, etc., and sit on rigid, low friction mounting points convenient to the suspension, accessible for change or adjustment, with freedom for the lever arms/blades to move full travel without fouling.

The normal link from bar to suspension has small spherical joints at each end with left/right threads to allow accurate setting of length without dismantling. The mountings will decide the length of bar, suitably designed to permit different diameters to be rapidly installed, and the maximum/minimum space for any adjustable lever arm. Blades show one of their many advantages here, needing no extra space for adjustment in length as they need only to be rotated from vertical to horizontal within their own width.

An elegant way of fitting a bar very strongly yet permitting complete and rapid change to a different diameter is used on Van Diemen cars. The bar has a projecting spigot at each end which fits a small ball bearing itself held in a rigidly located split alloy housing. Any alternative with the same spigots, irrespective of diameter or whether tubed or solid will go straight into the same mounts.

We now have our length and lever arm dimensions, and given a stiffness requirement can at last calculate the bar dimensions in diameter and wall thickness to get what we want. It is taken that the bar in serious racing machinery will be of tube because it always has a weight/stiffness ratio advantage over solid metal. Complete details of this approach together with all the formulae and example figures for a typical single seater will be found in Chapter Eight.

There are varied opinions on what constitutes the balance required but a reasonable first target is that there will be no weight transfer from front to back or vice versa in a steady state corner. Knowing what bar alterations can then provide in modifying front or rear roll stiffness (or both) track testing will be the basis of final refinements.

Yet again, as in the notable case of the roll centre, this is a static situation on paper, or at best in a steady state with our mount hurtling round a corner of constant radius at a fixed speed. We all know this never happens. Racing cars are always having the accelerator or brake pedal pressed firmly downwards upsetting the centre of gravity, weight transfer or roll forces at one end or the other, often in very quick succession, trying to skew roll all those neatly predicted forces and points in space.

Only practice, driver and development engineer talent and a responsive vehicle will contrive to put the finishing touches. Like charm, some have a large measure to start with, some acquire and polish it, while some unfortunates never ever manage to understand what it is they lack.

Steering

Already considered in Chapter 4 - especially the need for lightness (massive physical effort at anything rarely makes for delicacy of touch) - but we are now considering how and where to locate the rack and pinion. There are two major considerations: avoiding and protecting the driver's legs, whether in normal racing or in an accident, and avoidance of bump steer.

Bump steer, a well known phrase but not always clearly understood, is the phenomena in which either or both front wheels will start pointing themselves in varying directions as they rise and fall without the driver turning the steering wheel. This can be every bit as bad as it sounds, and at its worst will introduce straight line 'darting' instability, and highly unwanted uncertainty in cornering feel. Only after the location of all the front suspension pivots has been finalised can the rack position and its required length be

Methods of determining the best position for the rack and pinion.

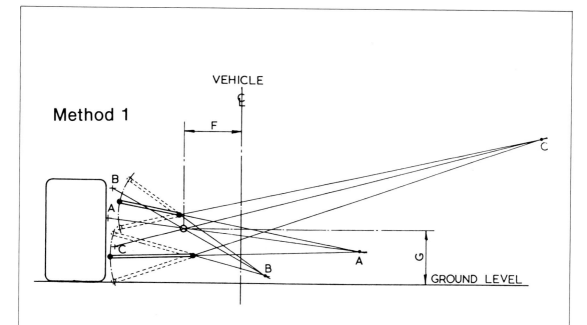

Method 1

VEHICLE ℄

F

C

A

B

C

A

B

G

GROUND LEVEL

Correct R & P Length = F × 2

Correct R & P Height = G

Method 3

R & P ball ends coincide exactly with top link inboard pickups with track rods lying parallel to top link.

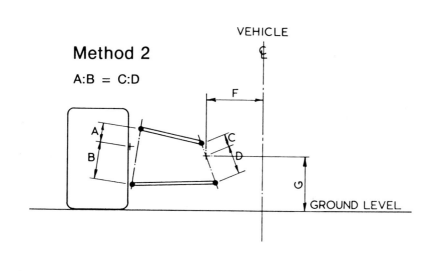

Method 2

A:B = C:D

VEHICLE ℄

F

A

B

C

D

G

GROUND LEVEL

determined.

Yet again words fall short of pictures in explaining how this is achieved and two different approaches are illustrated. In practice, methods 1 and 2 can give slightly different results and clearly both cannot be right. However, in practice, there are two further fine adjustment methods that remove the small errors that will almost inevitably be found when the car is finally assembled.

The first is altering the height of the rack. It is important if at all possible to provide some vertical adjustment in its position, usually with slotted holes for the mounting clamp bolts. This is the best way, but adjustment in the height of the track rod end by variable shims above and below is capable of bringing bump steer into the region of plus/minus 0.020 in. A third and simplest approach is a rack with end pivots that coincide exactly with the top wishbone mounting points.

The usual simple toe-in/out gauge used to check tracking is not really accurate enough for a serious attack on bump steer, and even the optical beam variety is extremely laborious because of the need for continually resetting its positions as the wheel moves during bump and rebound. A gauge both simpler to use and with a high degree of accuracy is illustrated. To use it you remove or disconnect the spring so the hub can rise and fall freely. Support the car on blocks, fit the hub plate and lock the hub against turning by a small wooden wedge. Rest the pointer (A) against the plate and zero the dial gauge with the wheels at standard ride height and parallel (zero toe in/out).

You can now move the hub up and down in quarter inch increments with a small jack, checking variations in or out from full bump to full droop on the dial. Depending on the figures you are, of course, writing down, adjustment to the rack height or bar length will be:

Bump	Droop	Rack adjustment
Toe-in	Toe-out	Raise forward R&P
		Lower rearward R&P
Toe-out	Toe-in	Lower forward R&P
		Lower rearward R&P
Toe-out	Toe-out	Lengthen bar (fwd)
		Shorten bar (rwd)
Toe-in	Toe-in	Shorten bar (fwd)
		Lengthen bar (rwd)

In every case of alteration whether in the height of the rack or the length of the bar, the track rods should be re-adjusted

Bump/steer gauge, as mentioned in the text. As upright rises/falls (using jack under suspension after removal of spring/damper unit) plate will indicate on dial gauge whether toe in/out is occuring and magnitude of change in series of steps from maximum bump to maximum droop.

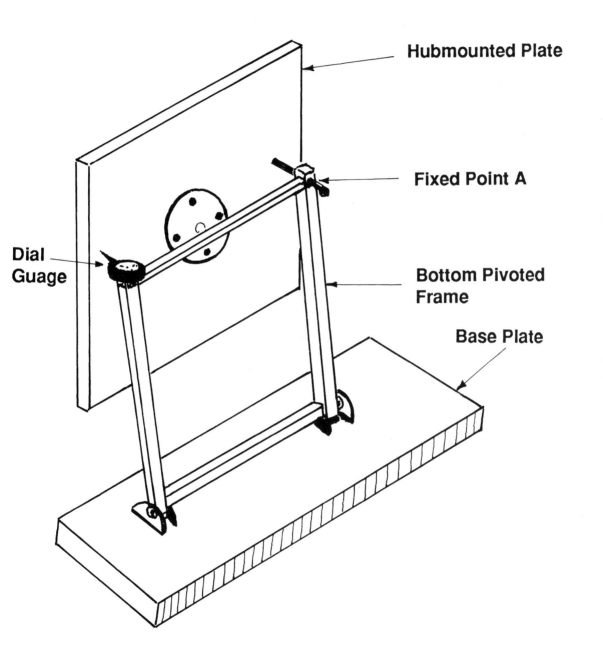

Hubmounted Plate

Fixed Point A

Dial
Guage

Bottom Pivoted
Frame

Base Plate

and the wheels brought back to parallel at ride height.

Corrections in the height of the track rod end itself are not nearly so clearcut, and for reasons connected with the sometimes complex arcs of the top and bottom wishbones (sometimes set on skewed axes, relative to the car centre-line) do somewhat unexpected things. However, tenacious experiment with shims will succeed if you keep at it. Just in case you thought that had dealt with bump steer for good, remember that an adjustment in caster angle effectively lowers a rear mounted steering arm and raises a forward mounted one, and thus the track rod end attached to it.

If caster angle alterations are planned in the field do the experiments on your flat floor in the workshop , making a note of the shims or alterations that must be made to keep bump-steer well out of the picture. You can then make the needed modifications rapidly without any need for checking at the track.

All the foregoing will perhaps give a small hint of why cars in some teams appear to have some miraculous edge over the opposition. In this area and others they not only know what they are doing, but how and why.

Weight
Transfer

...the final touch

8

```
--------------------------------------------------------------------------------
ROLL BARS, ROLL RESISTANCE & WEIGHT TRANSFER          dsg          Date ;(mm/dd/yy)   5/ 1/87
--------------------------------------------------------------------------------
       Client  :  R. Soles Esq.                        :                         : Notes
       Car Type :  Squirmer Mk 1                        :
--------------------------------------------------------------------------------
```

	FRONT	REAR		FRONT	REAR	TOTAL	
Total Corner Wt :	200	360	Total Wt :	400	720	1,120	lbs
Unsprung -"- Wt :	50	60	Wt Distribution :	35.7%	64.3%		
Axle Height :	10.00	12.00	Unsprung Wt :	100	120	220	lbs
			Sprung Wt :	300	600	900	lbs
			Sprung Wt Distrib :	33.3%	66.7%		
CG Height (agl) :	13.00	16.00	Mean CG Ht :			15.00	in
RC Height (agl) :	1.50	3.00	Mean RC Ht :			2.50	in
Track :	58.00	55.00	Mean Track :			56.00	in
			Roll Couple :			12.50	in
			Roll Moment (1g) :			11,250	lbs/in

Roll Bar Dimensions

	FRONT	REAR		FRONT	REAR		
Diameter :	.75	.75					
Bore :	.65	.65					
Length :	36.00	14.00	Angular Rate :	75	194		lb/in/deg
Lever Length :	7.00	7.00	Linear Rate :	88	227		lbs/in

Roll Resistance, Bars

	FRONT	REAR		FRONT	REAR		
Wheel Movement :	1.00	1.00	Eff. Fract. LA :	.90	.36		
Bar PU Movement :	.95	.60	Bar Roll Res. :	4,676	4,313		lb/in/deg

Roll Resistance, Springs

	FRONT	REAR		FRONT	REAR		
Spring Rate :	175	400	Eff. LA Ratio :	1.78	2.78		: 1
Wheel Movement :	1.00	1.00	Wheel Rate :	98.44	144.00		lbs/in
Damper Movement :	.75	.60	Spring Roll Res. :	2,890	3,801		lb/in/deg

Overall Roll Resistance

	FRONT	REAR	TOTAL	
Total :	7,565	8,114	15,679	lb/in/deg
Distribution :	48.3%	51.7%		

Dynamic Weight Transfer at 1g

	FRONT	REAR	TOTAL	
Unsprung Weight :	17.24	26.18	43.42	lbs
Via Roll Axis :	7.76	32.73	40.49	lbs
Sprung Weight :	96.93	103.96	200.89	lbs
Total Transferred :	121.93	162.87	284.80	lbs

Dynamic Weight Distribution at 1g

	FRONT	REAR	TOTAL	
F - R Wt Change :	29.97	(29.97)	.00	lbs
Revised Weights :	429.97	690.03	1,120	lbs
Wt Distribution :	38.4%	61.6%	5.4%	F <- R
Roll Angle at 1g :			.72	degrees

David Gould is one of the most successful of Britain's amateur racing car designers. Each of his cars have followed three maxima - the highest possible rigidity, careful suspension design and a major step forward in concept over the previous design. His most recent car is a full honeycomb monocoque, that despite being built in the wooden garage beside his semi, took the British Hillclimb Championship from the most formidable of opposition in its first season.

Some idea of the effort and thought that goes into Gould's design approach, as well as a wealth of practical guidance, is reflected in the following paper.

LATERAL WEIGHT TRANSFER AND ROLL RESISTANCE, BY DAVID GOULD.

I am sure many of us have stood about in assorted Paddocks, Beer Tents and Bars discussing with our fellow competitors the relative merits of "soft" or "hard" roll bars, transferring weight to or from the front or rear suspension, and so forth, our dialogue being liberally peppered with impressive phrases such as Roll Couple, Roll Moments, Fractional Lever Arms, and the like. I am equally sure that almost as many of us would have difficulty putting our hands on our hearts and swearing that we were fully aware of the major factors involved, or that we could quantify their individual and total magnitudes with any hope of the results standing even the most informal scrutiny.

One of the reasons for this situation prevailing is the lack of comprehensive text books covering the subject. Almost all the written matter available appears to fall into one of two categories, either the author is a professional engineer writing in mechanical engineering terms, thus making assumptions regarding the reader's knowledge that leaves us, as amateurs, more confused after reading such articles than before, or the subject is so broadly discussed that scarcely a clue is given which is of use to us.

In an attempt to clear away some of the mystique surrounding the subject an effort will be made to explain the basic principles at work and to introduce a fairly painless method of arriving at figures which will reveal some of the more important forces at work and their relationship with one another.

Weight transfer

We all know that roll bars influence weight transfer and that weight transfer is somehow connected with roll centres, it would therefore seem appropriate to start at the common denominator. To understand how weight is transferred we must first apportion the various components which make up the total weight according to their position in the vehicle.

We will give codes to the terms which will be used in the various formulae and these are listed on pages 212/213. In addition, a set of data, not completely dissimilar to that of a medium sized hillclimb single seater, will be used to provide examples and these basic values also appear on pages 212/213 with an illustration. A cornering force of 1G is assumed throughout.

Before we begin we need to know the weights involved and their positions relative to one another, these can be calculated or measured as follows:

WF or WR = Total weight on front or rear axle line.

UWF or UWR = The weight of the unsprung components, eg. wheels, tyres, brakes, wishbones, uprights, etc., at the front or rear of the car.

UGF or UGR = The height of the centre of gravity of the front or rear unsprung mass; this is usually similar to the radius of the tyre.

TF or TR = The distance between the centre lines of the front or rear wheels.

WF - UWR = SWF, front sprung weight; WR - UWR = SWR, rear sprung weight; SWF + SWR = SW, total sprung weight.

By way of example,

WF 400lbs. - UWF 100lbs. = 300lbs. SWF
WR 720lbs. - UWR 120lbs. = 600lbs. SWR
300 + 600 = 900lbs. SW

Armed with the above we can now commence calculating the first of three types of weight transfer.

Unsprung weight transfer

The following formulae will calculate the unsprung weight transfers at the front and rear, respectively,

UWF x UGF ÷ TF = UtF (Front unsprung weight transfer)
100 x 10 ÷ 58 = 17.24 lbs.
UWR x UGR ÷ TR = UtR (Rear unsprung weight transfer)
120 x 12 ÷ 55 = 26.18lbs.

Obviously, the greater the weight and height the more weight transfer there will be and, conversely, the greater the track the less the weight transfer. Equally obvious, short of chopping the car about or drilling holes all over the place there is nothing we can do to modify this constituent of total weight transfer without major re-design.

Weight transfer via the roll centres

This is the element of the sprung mass which is reacted into the outer tyres directly through the roll centres, and is calculated thus,
SWF x CF ÷ TF = CtF (front weight transfer via the roll centres)
300 x 1.5 ÷ 58 = 7.76lbs.
SWR x CR ÷ TR = CtR (rear weight transfer via the roll centres)
600 x 3.0 ÷ 55 = 32.73lbs.

As can be seen, this element of weight transfer can be increased or decreased simply by raising or lowering the height of the roll centre at one or other end of the car without having any direct effect on the other end. In practical racing terms this is usually a small proportion of the total Transferable Weight.

Weight transfer via the sprung mass

This is the mass of the car which rolls around the axis between the front and rear roll centres and as such is the part of the vehicle whose roll is resisted by the springs and roll bars. It is therefore the area of weight transfer offering the greatest reward for our attention; in typical fashion, however, it is the most difficult to understand and calculate.

For proper comprehension we need to introduce the concept of The Mass Centroid. When visualising the sprung mass we must never think in terms of front and rear axles, front and rear weights, front and rear heights or front and rear roll centres if we are ever to grasp a full understanding.

Sitting somewhere near the middle of the car is a mass whose centre is the Centre of Gravity of the entire sprung weight of the car. It knows nothing about front and rear tracks, front and rear roll centres or front and rear CoGs. What it does know about is its own track, its own roll centre and its own CoG. We will call these the Mean Track, the Mean Roll Centre and the Mean CoG.

Before we can calculate them we need to find the proportion of the total sprung weight resting on one of the axles. The rear axle is calculated as follows,

SWR ÷ SW = WDR

600 ÷ 900 = 0.66 recurring.

This indicates that the sprung mass CoG is located at a point two thirds of the distance from the front to the rear axle; somewhere just in front of the engine.

Having obtained the above we now know the whereabouts of the centre of the sprung mass along the wheelbase of the car, and can thus calculate its mean track, mean roll centre and mean CoG, using the same proportion and based on the known front and rear measurements at each end of the car.

((TR - TF) x WDR) + TF = TM (mean track)

((CR - CF) x WDR) + CF = CM (mean roll centre)

eg;

((55 - 58) x 0.66r) + 58 = 56 inch mean track

((3.0 - 1.5) x 0.66r) + 1.5 = 2.5 inch mean roll centre

Before we can complete the exercise and calculate mean CoG we need to know the height of the CoG of the sprung mass at the front and rear axle lines. These can be extremely difficult to measure and a process of deduction from the known location of the major items which comprise the sprung weight is often the preferred method of assessing this information.

((SGR - SGF) x WDR) + SGF = GM

((16 - 13) x 0.66r) + 13 = 15 inch mean CoG height

All that is required now is the length of the lever arm (or moment) between the mean roll centre about which our sprung mass will rotate and the mean CoG. This is calculated as follows,

GM - CM = LM, mean roll moment

15 - 2.5 = 12.5 inch mean roll moment

We now have all the information we need to calculate the Sprung Weight Transfer and the formula is,

SW x LM ÷ TM = St, total sprung weight transfer

900 x 12.5 ÷ 56 = 200.89lbs. total sprung weight transfer.

It can be seen that the length of LM is dependent on the height and slope of the roll axis; the higher the roll axis the more weight transferred via the roll centres and, consequently, the less weight transferred through the springs.

A little research with a calculator will convince you that these two methods of transferring weight (via the roll centres or via the springs) precisely counterbalance each other and the total amount of weight transferred, no matter which route it follows, always remains the same, ie. high roll centres leave less weight available to transfer via the springs, and vice versa.

Total weight transfer

This is now obtainable by adding all the above together thus,

UtF + UtR + CtF + CtR + St = Wt

17.24 + 26.18 + 7.76 + 32.73 + 200.89 = 284.8lbs. total weight transfer.

One might, at this point, wonder why anyone would bother going to all the trouble of calculating weight transfer in such a complex manner when it is now obvious that the total amount of weight transferable in a given situation is completely predetermined by vehicle dimensions.

Look again at the formula for total weight transfer given above. If you have been paying attention you will have noticed that the term in the equation "St" (sprung weight transfer), unlike all the preceding terms, was not calculated separately for the front and rear suspensions. This is because, while its share of the total weight transferred is inversely proportional to the amount of weight transferred via the roll centres, its front and rear distribution is not controlled by any of the factors we have considered so far.

The Golden Rule is:

"The ratio of front to rear sprung weight weight transfer is directly proportional to the ratio of front to rear roll resistance".

In other words, the end of the car which is stiffest will receive the major part of sprung transferred weight and its exact share will be governed by its stiffness relative to the stiffness of the other end of the car.

Roll Resistance

Once again, nothing in life is simple, and if we are to take advantage of our new found ability to apply sprung weight transfer to either end of the car we will need to be able to determine how stiff our front and rear suspension really is.

We will now deliberate on the factors which contribute to roll stiffness, ie. springs, roll bars, their strengths and the leverages with which they applied. Let us begin with one of the oldest roll resisting devices of all.

Springs

In addition to the Spring Rate we need to know the ratio of wheel movement to spring movement, this needs to be measured with as much accuracy as possible as this value will be squared in our calculation and obviously any error will also be squared.

The ratio is found by measuring the exact amount of movement of the spring for a given amount of wheel movement. One inch is a convenient dimension and is used in our example. One practical method to obtain the measurement is as follows. Block up the chassis at its normal ride height and, with the springs removed, measure the distance between the upper and lower spring location collars then, without disturbing anything else, place a spacer of known thickness between the tyre and the ground and remeasure the distance between the spring collars. The thickness of the spacer (wheel movement) divided by the difference between the two measurements of spring collar distance (spring movement) is the ratio we are seeking.

We can now proceed to calculate the roll resistance of the springs as follows,

$(SF \div (WmF \div SmF)^2) \times TF^2 \div 2 \times Pi \div 180 = ArF$, roll resistance of front springs

$(SR \div (WmR \div SmR)^2) \times TR^2 \div 2 \times Pi \div 180 = ArR$, roll resistance of rear springs

$(175 \div (1.0 \div 0.75)^2) \times 58^2 \div 2 \times Pi \div 180 = 2,889.77$ inch lbs. per degree roll resistance of front springs

$(400 \div (1.00 \div 0.60)^2) \times 55^2 \div 2 \times Pi \div 180 = 3,801.33$ inch lbs. per degree roll resistance of rear springs

The term "Pi ÷ 180" in the above formulae was included to convert the result to units of inch lbs. per degree; omitting this will produce and answer in units of lb. inch lbs. per radian; as a radian is about 57.3 degrees it is far too large a unit to be convenient or practical in suspension calculations.

Roll bars

Unlike springs, roll bars are not usually marked with their rate and it is therefore necessary to calculate this value before we can begin to find their effect on roll resistance. Again, very careful measurement is required for the outside and inside (if the bar is tubular) diameters, as these values are multiplied to the fourth power in the equation. To begin, let us find the angular rate of our bars, ie., the force necessary to twist them a given amount.

Angular Rate

Both the bars used in our example are manufactured from 0.75" diameter x 0.05" wall tubes, the front and rear lengths are 36" and 14" respectively.

19,700 x (OD^4- ID^4) ÷ Bar length = Angular Rate in inch lbs. per degree

19,700 x (0.75^4- 0.65^4) ÷ 36 = 75.46 inch lbs. per degree (front bar)

19,700 x (0.75^4- 0.65^4) ÷ 14 = 194.05 inch lbs. per degree (rear bar)

The figure of 19,700 is a constant derived from the average modulus of elasticity for steel. For solid bar, omit the internal dimension "- ID^4" term and simply use OD^4

Note that the angular rate is exactly inversely proportional to length, ie. double the length = half the strength.

Linear Rate

We must now find the effect of the length of the roll bar lever arms. This dimension is measured at right angles to the axis of the bar and is the distance from the roll bar push rod pick up point to the centre line of the roll bar; in our example we will assume that both front and rear bars have 7" levers.

Angular Rate ÷ (Lever length^2 x Pi ÷ 180) = Roll bar rate in inch lbs.

BF = 75.46 ÷ (7^2 x Pi ÷ 180) = 88.24 inch lbs. (Front roll bar rate)

BR = 194.05 ÷ (7^2 x Pi ÷ 180) = 226.90 inch lbs. (Rear roll bar rate)

Now that we know the roll bar rates we can proceed to find their effect on roll resistance. Again we need to measure the proportion of wheel movement to roll bar pick up movement and this can be achieved using similar procedures to those outlined in the section on springs above. We can now calculate as follows,

BF x (WmF x BmF)^2 x TF^2 x Pi ÷ 180 = BrF, roll resistance of front bar

BR x (WmR x BmR)^2 x TR^2 x Pi ÷ 180 = BrR, roll resistance of rear bar

88.24 x (1.00 x 0.95)^2 x 58^2 x Pi ÷ 180 = 4,675.69 inch lbs. per degree roll resistance of front bar

$226.90 \times (1.00 \times 0.60)^2 \times 55^2 \times Pi \div 180 = 4{,}312.61$ inch lbs. per degree roll resistance of rear bar

Distribution

Having now calculated all the elements contributing to the total roll resistance of the car, we can now proceed to split our sprung weight transfer between front and rear suspensions. First we will add the spring and bar resistances together,

ArF + BrF = Fr, front roll resistance
ArR + BrR = Rr, rear roll resistance
$2{,}889.77 + 4{,}675.69 = 7{,}565.46$ inch lbs. per degree front roll resistance
$3{,}801.33 + 4{,}312.61 = 8{,}113.94$ inch lbs. per degree rear roll resistance

You will recall the distribution of sprung weight transfer is proportional to the ratio of front to rear roll resistance, therefore,

Fr ÷ (Fr + Rr) = DrF
$7{,}565.46 \div (7{,}565.46 + 8{,}113.94) = 0.483$

Thus, the roll resistance of the front suspension is 48.3% of the total roll resistance of the vehicle, the remainder must be at the rear and is therefore,

1 - DrF = DrR
$1 - 0.483 = 0.517$ (or 51.7%)

The dynamic weight transfer applicable to each end of the vehicle can now be found by using these proportions in the following formulae,

(St x DrF) + CtF + UtF = WtF, total weight transferred to the outer front wheel
(St x DrR) + CtR + UtR = WtR, total weight transferred to the outer rear wheel
$(200.89 \times 0.483) + 7.76 + 17.24 = 122$ lbs. total weight transferred to the outer front wheel
$(200.89 \times 0.517) + 32.73 + 26.18 = 163$ lbs. total weight transferred to the outer rear wheel

The amount of weight transferred from one end to the other as a result of our roll bars, springs, leverages and roll centre positions can be found by calculating as follows,

WtF - ((SW x (1 - WDR) x LM ÷ TM) + UtF + CtF) = Weight to or from front
WtR - ((SW x WDR x LM ÷ TM) + UtR + CtR) = Weight to or from rear
$122 - ((900 \times (1 - 0.66r) \times 12.5 \div 56) + 17.24 + 7.76) = +30$ lbs

front

163 - ((900 x 0.66r x 12.5 ÷ 56) + 26.18 + 32.73) = -30 lbs rear

In other words, when the car is cornering at 1G we have made the rear of it 30 lbs. lighter and the front 30 lbs. heavier, a change in the overall weight distribution of about 5.4% towards the front. It is clear that far larger changes can be achieved by using softer or stiffer bars at either end to modify the proportion of roll resistance and consequent sprung weight transfer.

Roll angles

The sprung mass is, by definition, the only part of the car which is suspended on springs, and is therefore the only part of the car which can roll. The amount of roll at a given cornering force is therefore determined by the total weight of the sprung mass, its height above the roll axis (Mean Roll Moment) and the total roll resistance of the car (the sum of the front and rear roll resistances). To find the roll angle of the chassis in a 1G corner we can therefore calculate as follows,

(SW x LM) ÷ (Fr + Rr) = Roll Angle

(900 x 12.5) ÷ (7,565.46 + 8,113.94) = 0.72 degrees

Notice that, as the roll axis height, which can be adjusted by raising or lowering the roll centres at either end of the car, controls the value of LM, we can reduce the amount of roll by raising the roll centre heights and vice versa.

Summary

A final sobering thought. All the above calculations assume a totally rigid chassis which does not actually exist. They also assume friction-free mountings, geometric perfection in linkages, non-flex pick-up points and rigid lever arms, all of which are either rare or impossible in current practical terms.

This should not deter you because everybody else faces the same difficulties, but may have even less idea of what they are doing or in which direction they are proceeding. That can only be to your advantage.

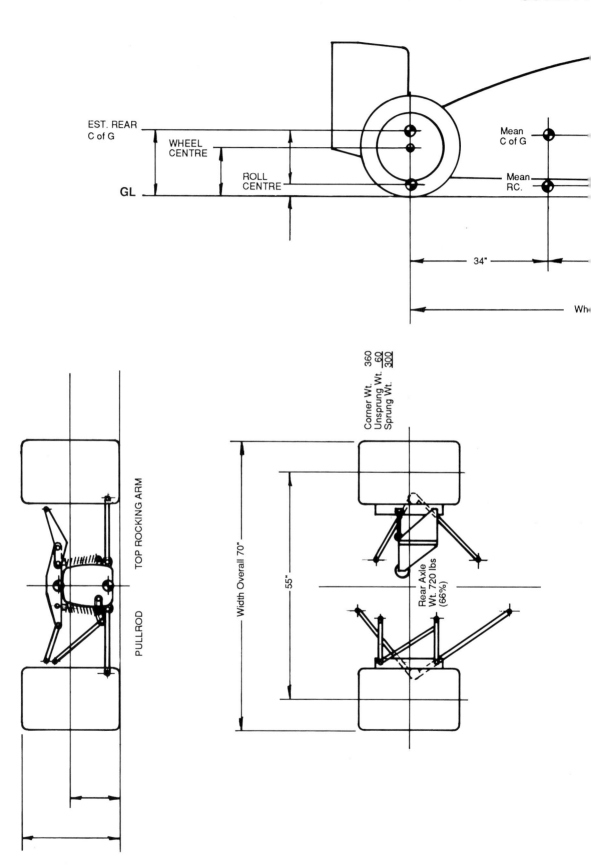

EST. REAR
C of G

WHEEL
CENTRE

ROLL
CENTRE

GL

Mean
C of G

Mean
RC.

34"

Wh

TOP ROCKING ARM

PULLROD

Corner Wt. 360
Unsprung Wt. 60
Sprung Wt. 300

Width Overall 70"

55"

Rear Axle
Wt. 720 lbs
(66%)

'PE (EXAMPLE)

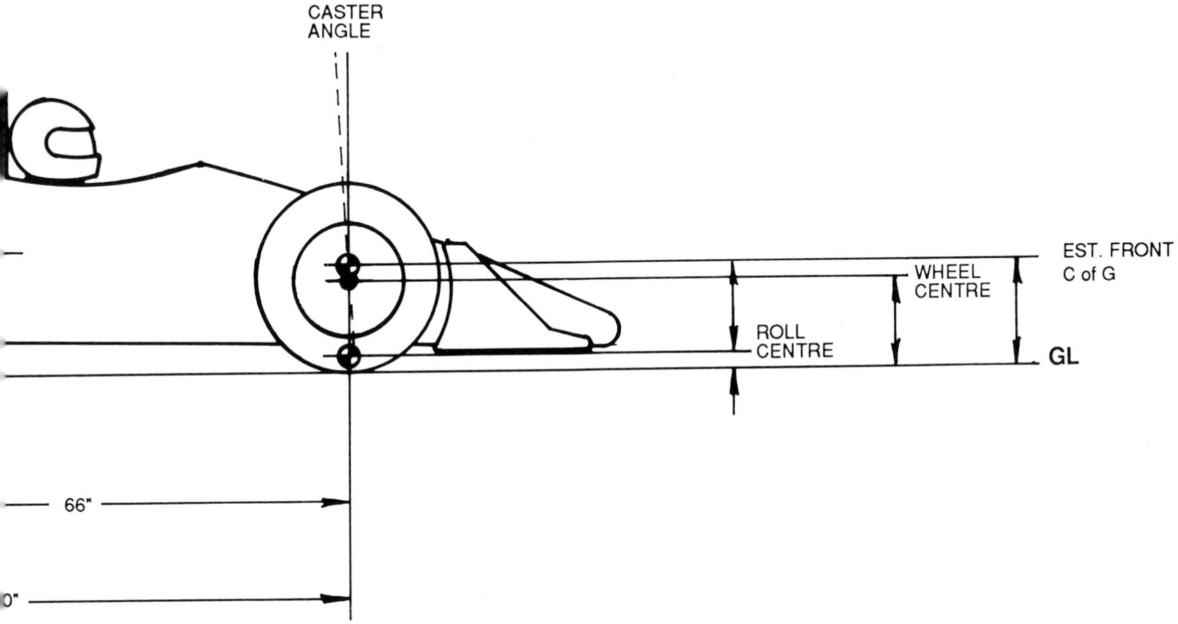

CASTER
ANGLE

WHEEL
CENTRE

EST. FRONT
C of G

ROLL
CENTRE

GL

66"

0"

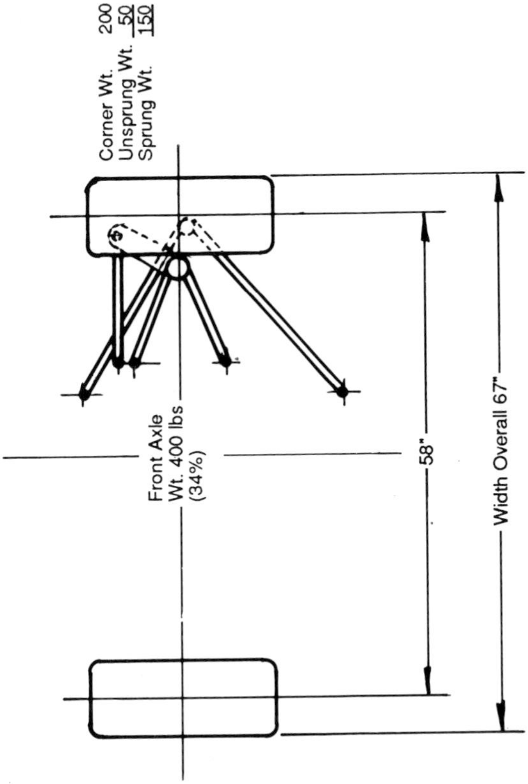

Corner Wt.　200
Unsprung Wt.　50
Sprung Wt.　150

Front Axle
Wt. 400 lbs
(34%)

58"

Width Overall 67"

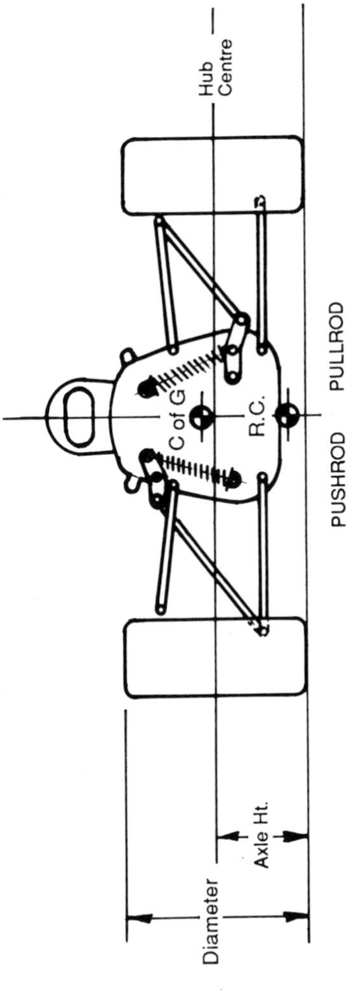

Hub
Centre

C of G

R.C.

PUSHROD

PULLROD

Diameter

Axle Ht.

Schedule of Terms

Measured Example Data

W	= Total weight of car and driver	1,120 lbs.
WF	= Total weight, front	400 lbs.
WR	= Total weight, rear	720 lbs.
UWF	= Total unsprung weight, front	100 lbs.
UWR	= Total unsprung weight, rear	120 lbs.
UGF	= Unsprung CoG height, front	10 inches
UGR	= Unsprung CoG height, rear	12 inches
TF	= Track, front	58 inches
TR	= Track, rear	55 inches
CF	= Height of front roll centre	1.50 inches
CR	= Height of rear roll centre	3.00 inches
SGF	= Sprung CoG height, front	13 inches
SGR	= Sprung CoG height, rear	16 inches
SF	= Front spring rate	175 lbs.
SR	= Rear spring rate	400 lbs.
Wm	= Front wheel movement	1.00 inches
WmR	= Rear wheel movement	1.00 inches
SmF	= Relative front spring movement	0.75 inches
SmR	= Relative rear spring movement	0.60 inches
BmF	= Relative front roll bar pick up movement	0.95 inches
BmR	= Relative rear roll bar pick up movement	0.60 inches

Calculated Example Data

SWF	= Total sprung weight, front	300 lbs.
SWR	= Total sprung weight, rear	600 lbs.
SW	= Total sprung weight	900 lbs.
UtF	= Unsprung weight transfer, front	17.24 lbs.
UtR	= Unsprung weight transfer, rear	26.18 lbs.
CtF	= Weight transferred via front roll centre	7.76 lbs.
CtR	= Weight transferred via rear roll centre	32.73 lbs.
WDR	= Proportion of sprung weight on rear axle	66%
TM	= Mean track of sprung weight	56 inches
CM	= Mean roll centre of sprung weight	2.5 inches
GM	= Mean CoG of sprung weight	15 inches
LM	= Mean roll moment of sprung weight	12.5 inches
St	= Weight transferred due the the sprung mass	200.89 lbs.
Wt	= Total weight transfer	284.84 lbs.

ArF = Front roll resistance due to springs..2,889.77 inch lbs. per deg.
ArR = Rear roll resistance due to springs...3,801.33 inch lbs. per deg.
BF = Front roll bar rate....................................88.24 inch lbs.
BR = Rear roll bar rate.................................... 226.9 inch lbs.
BrF = Front roll resistance due to bars........4,675.69 inch lbs. per deg.
BrR = Rear roll resistance due to bars.........4,312.61 inch lbs. per deg.
Fr = Total front roll resistance...................7,565.46 inch lbs. per deg.
Rr = Total rear roll resistance....................8,113.94 inch lbs. per deg.
DrF = Front roll stiffness,
       proportional to total.................................48.3 %
DrR = Rear roll stiffness,
       proportional to total.................................51.7 %
WtF = Total front weight transfer.......................122 lbs.
WtR = Total rear weight transfer........................163 lbs.

APPENDICES

The String Computer

Not everyone, even in these days of an Amstrad or IBM checking the laundry list and pantry stock levels of baked beans, will have the resources or expertise to use computer techniques to design a wishbone suspension that has a fighting chance of working reasonably well and in a known manner. Do not despair.

When friend and fellow designer Richard Blackmore and I were first struggling to bring the Terrapin from an idea to racing reality, we desperately needed some way in which to analyse what an existing suspension might be doing and/ or create our own with known objectives. The result was an analogue computer, generally known as a working model. It was, and is, a deceptively simple device for such a complex subject, but you have to start somewhere and even the mathematical model approach through current computers will only give you answers - hundreds of thousands of them if you require it to. You still have to ask the right questions, and then sort the wheat from the chaff in the answers.

Eschewing the electronic approach, the String Computer does not demand either mathematical or drawing office skills. A full scale version might be ideal but half-scale (my own) is rather more practical, especially for the longer Swing Axle Lengths. The photographs show its component parts and how it is actually operated. Cut the composite parts from hardboard or thin plywood. These are:

a) Baseboard with ground level, bounce/droop markings, car centre line with angles of roll from the vertical axis, wheel centre line with angles of negative/ positive camber and ground level line, also with angles of roll from the horizontal.

b) Two calibrated strips which will represent the wishbones (A-arms).

c) The "chassis" board marked with vertical and horizontal dimensions from centre line and ground level. The significance of this item is that it will be free to rotate about the roll centre, once this has been identified, and thus permit roll to be inserted into the action of the model.

d) An outline of the wheel and tyre/upright/pick-up points for the vehicle you are designing or analysing.

e) Ball of string, sundry pins and screws and a wire hook with a handle.

The method of operation is as follows:

i) With wheel vertical and set on its centre line, pin the wishbones into their chosen positions, then align the string along the top and bottom links, and finally bring it back from their intersection point to the contact point of the wheel with the ground.

ii) Insert the Roll Centre pin where the string cuts the centre line of the car.

iii) Rotate the "chassis" board through one degree while keeping the wheel at ground level.

iv) Note all the results.

v) Reset the string, and Roll Centre pin if necessary, and increase roll to two degrees.

The effect of the model is to reproduce much more realistically what actually happens to a wheel and tyre and the roll centre in a corner rather than the simpler and more conventional movement of it simply rising and falling. This last can, of course, be checked quite simply by raising and lowering the wheel while keeping the chassis board horizontal (ie, parallel to the ground).

You now commence a series of experiments, varying the dimensions and locations of the top and bottom links in search of your chosen movements and inclinations of the wheel, together with, so far as possible a fixed roll centre.

Work within practical limits of bump and droop, which will be considerably less on a single seater than on a saloon or some sports cars. Don't forget that you do not want to end up with ideal suspension points that are either unsupportable in thin air or lie in the middle of the driver's calf muscle.

Although this might sound a little laborious and time consuming, you will soon find that visible trends appear, with certain alterations producing particular results. And it has to be mega-quicker than trying to draw it all...

Even should you not be planning to go further than reading the foregoing, it will, perhaps, give a flavour of the questions and decisions in this area alone that face a designer up against the need to produce a winner - or find a new job. He has also to choose between a multiplicity of targets, many in total opposition to each other. These may be summed up in bare outline as:

1. Roll Centre.

More than a little disagreement about how vital is its accurate location but a personal view with nothing convincing to alter it over quite a few years is "absolutely vital". It is common ground that a car in roll under a cornering G force

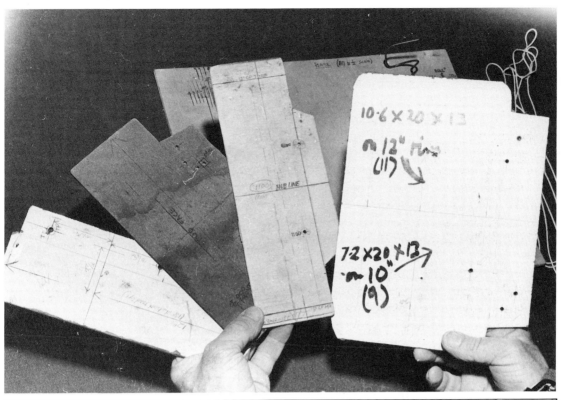

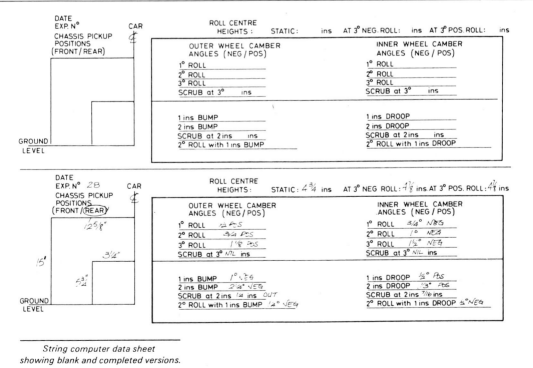

String computer data sheet showing blank and completed versions.

must be rotating about some point in space. The dissent is usually about where it might be, if it has moved from a theoretical position and why. These arguments are absolutely no reason not to make strenuous attempts to locate and pin it down. Ignorance of at least an idea of the location of the front and rear roll centres, both statically and dynamically will prevent any attempts at logical thought or modifications when you have problems.

Varying roll centres at each end of the car must result in varying loads and weight transfer front, back and diagonally under differing circumstances. A moment's thought about the possible result for the driver in a fast left-right flick would suggest he will be in next lap complaining bitterly and calling for immediate improvement.

Current thinking on roll centre heights is of the order of 2 ins. above ground level to 1 in. below at the lighter/lower end of the car, with 4 ins. above down to ground level at the other end. These figures normally give an inclined roll axis along the car tending to even out the various forces involved if nothing else, but are by no means a fixed approach. It is a free world.

So we will aim at a dynamically steady roll centre so far as it may be possible, or at the very least similar movement at each end of the car.

2. Outer wheel vertical in roll.
With the two outer tyres doing the major part of the work in accepting cornering forces, this gives the tyre contact patches their best chance in life. Many cars, from a Mini to a Formula One, do not do this at all well geometrically and need the wheels set with a negative camber so that roll pushes them out towards vertical.

3. Wheel angle in bump/droop.
In direct opposition to (2), this has become ever more important in heavy braking and acceleration with wide flat slicks. In both situations there is a tendency under pitch forces for wheels to go into bump at one end and droop at the other, doing grip no good at all. A number of experiments over the years saw tyre companies (Dunlop for the Mini, Pirelli for Toleman and Ferrari) producing assymetric tyres with radiussed inner shoulders to try and alleviate this.

4. Track variation (scrub).
This means that individual wheels will, under certain circumstances, follow a private wavy path rather than a straight line. Most important when running straight, but

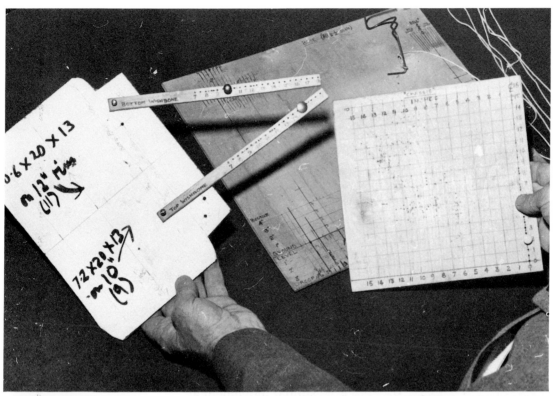

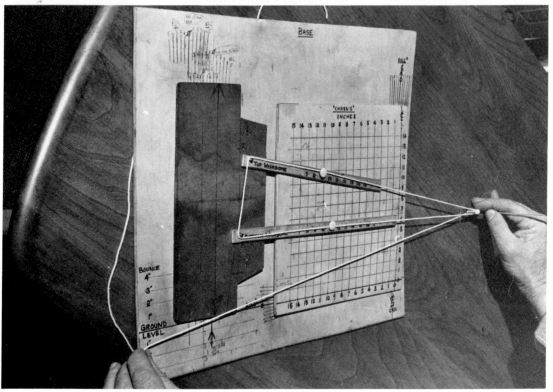

may be a contribution to momentary under or oversteer lurch on turn-in to a corner.

For the intrepid souls who are going ahead with the String (or any other) Computer, a few guidelines.

From scratch, work from a bottom link parallel to the ground and as long as practicable, combined with a top link two-thirds of the bottom running downhill from wheel to chassis at 15 degrees or so from horizontal. Note every experiment in detail as you carry it out. Trying to remember results and then compare them will only lead to a hopeless muddle.

Operations and effects:

1. Alteration of wishbone lengths - little major effect.

2. Lengthening both at once - often poorer.

3. Vertical movements of chassis mounts - major effects.

4. Scrub - rarely any problem in roll, can be serious in bump/droop.

5. "Skewed roll" - this may, for instance, combine 2 degrees of roll with 1 in. of bump on a front or rear wheel and can often give excellent results in terms of outer wheel angle.

All the variations we have considered here will, of course, be reduced by restricting the actual movement of the vehicle, a basic approach explored to the full both in Indy Cars and Formula One, giving minimal roll (controlled by extremely strong bars) and almost fixed ride heights (very hard suspension and high wheel frequencies). Having said this, one has to admit that several newest generation Formula One cars have only a modest front bar and no rear bar at all, the inference being that wheel frequencies are rising substantially and coils are taking back much of the task.

Such a simplistic method transfers much of the suspension's task onto the tyre carcase - and if you thought geometry was a little tricky it pales beside the mysteries of what a tyre may be doing in ten thousand situations, all different.

Here are some general pointers (irrespective of the method used).

1. Very short swing axle lengths (20 - 40 inches):

a) Roll centre (RC) generally high.

b) RC location generally good.

c) RC sideways movements at a minimum.

d) Very good wheel angle control in roll.

e) Camber variations in bump/droop very bad (almost linear with roll in some cases).

f) Bad performance in scrub.

2. Long swing axle lengths (70 - 180 inches):
a) RC low.
b) RC location reasonable, subject to (c).
c) RC can move considerable distances sideways due to the shallow angles involved.
d) Mediocre wheel angle control in roll (worst on inner wheel).
e) Camber alterations in bump/droop good.
f) Good performance in scrub.
3. Medium swing axle lengths (40 - 70 inches):
As might be expected, the results lie between short and long.
4. Ultra-long swing axle lengths (effectively out to infinity, with certain near-parallel designs):
a) RCs very low, at or below ground level.
b) RC location very good in vertical terms.
c) RC sideways movement can be very great, with a reversal from inside to outside of the corner possible due to the very narrow, near parallel angles.
d) Wheel angle control poor - may be near direct equivalency to car's roll angle.
e) Camber alterations in bump/droop very small.
f) Scrub - good.

Setting Up

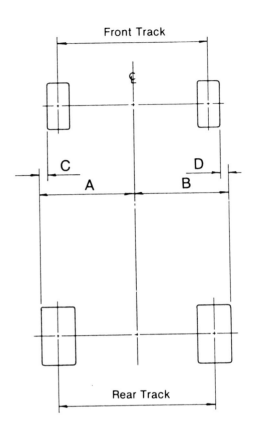

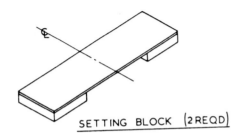

SETTING BLOCK (2 REQD)

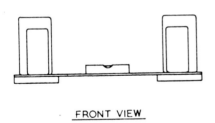

FRONT VIEW

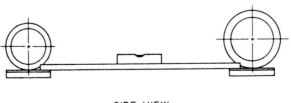

SIDE VIEW

Setting up a car is much less of a black art than a laborious long day, preferably with another person and relatively simple equipment. All it amounts to is making certain that all the wheels are pointing in the correct direction, especially relative to each other, that ride heights loaded are correct, roll bar links not under load, and the weight on each pair of tyres front or rear is split equally between them.

This is not only an essential basis on which to do any further development and testing, but should ensure that the car will have reasonable balance and handling first time out. It is by no means what you may end up with after experiment, but yet again, you have to start someplace.

Should you never have need or interest in doing this, it may still illuminate a walk round the pits seeing what the experts get up to.

1. First requirement is a level surface, or four level pads on which the wheels can rest. A decent concrete floor is by its manner of construction often excellent. Otherwise make four pads from plywood or hardboard, using a builder's spirit level and a long straight piece of wood or steel tube to level them before being numbered and a painted rectangle put on the floor to locate them for the future.

2. Make up four wooden blocks, two for the front and two for the rear, to ride height plus the thickness of the corner pad. Make four more that will sit on top of the first blocks, thick enough to hold all four wheels clear of the ground.

3. Roll car onto the pads, remove springs (but leave dampers, wishbones, etc. connected) and set on ride height blocks.

4. Set front caster angle. Use 3 degrees if you have no guide figure.

5. Set front and rear camber angles. Use vertical - 1 degree negative if no guide figures are available.

6. Check rack and pinion is parallel to the ground and at right angles to the centre line of the car. Measure its height. Disconnect track rod ends and centre rack bar in its housing.

7. Set toe-in on front wheels, and pointing straight ahead. Check lengths of track rods and adjust if necessary to fit between rack and steering arm. Reset steering wheel spokes if required.

8. Check that each rear wheel has the same toe relative to the centre line of the car, or is parallel to it. Run string or length of tube from each wheel to the front. "A" must equal "B".

9. Set rear toe. Normally toe-in. Use 3/8ths or 9mm. if no guide figure.

10. Check springs for pairs, both in free length and rate.

11. Remove dampers and check for pairs in open/closed lengths, any coding or part numbers, good end bushes or bearings, and no leaks. Set any adjustments to full soft. Grease and free adjustable collars and lock rings.

12. Refit all spring/dampers and lower car onto wheels without blocks.

13. Set correct ride heights, front and rear, with driver, all liquids and half tank of fuel.

14. Set corner weights to give two equal fronts and two equal rears. A "heavy" corner will need the spring platform lowering, and vice versa. Adjustments at one end will certainly affect the opposite end and may enforce a series of adjustments as you approach perfection.

15. Connect anti roll bar links adjusting the lengths so they do not exert any force whatever on the bars.

16. Check for bump-steer and adjust rack height and/or track rod end positions to eliminate or reduce to absolute minimum.

17. With car set at correct ride height and attitude measure and mark (or note adjustment dimensions) of front and rear wing angles of attack, what flap adjustment does, etc.

And make a note of everything, including all the later alterations which will probably be many.

Spherical Joints

Racing and other competition cars are full of spherical joints, often called 'Rose' or 'Ampeps' for short (from the manufacturers names). Joints with a 3/8ths in., or 10mm. shank are widely used in varying qualities, and some are compared in the table. The listing is based simply on radial load figures (lbs.) in order of strength. It is likely, but not certain, that the stronger the joints are, the more expensive. When buying it is worth checking not only different suppliers and manufacturers, but also a "strength/cost" ratio which may show that it is worthwhile to buy a smaller (but better material and stronger) joint rather than a larger but apparently cheaper one.

All the figures given an codes relate to 3/8ths in. x 3/8ths in. male joints. Female strength figures are normally slightly better than male. Axial strength figures (trying to push the ball out sideways) may be as low as 10% of the radial figure so use a big safety washer if the situation warrants it.

Code	Outer housing and finish	Ball and finish	Interliner	Radial load
RMR 6	Stainless	Stainless hardened through	PTFE/fibre	9850
RMX 6	Chrome Moly cad. plated	1% chrome, chrome plated	Aluminium/ bronze	9589
RCA 06	Stainless	Stainless hardened through	PTFE/fibre "Type R"	7150
RMC 6NU	Carbon steel phosphated	1% carb. chrome chrome plated	PTFE/fibre	7070
RBJ 73	Nickel chrome moly phosphated	1% carb. chrome chrome plated	None	6300
AMPEP 2185P	Med. carbon, low alloy. Phosphated	Med chrome, low alloy, chromed	"Fibreglide" PTFE/fibre	5242
RC6H	Carbon steel phosphated	Stainless thru, hardened	PTFE/fibre "Type R"	4420
RM6	Carbon steel cad. plated	1% carb. chrome plated	Navel bronze/ sintered copper	2450
RMP 6U	Carbon steel phosphated	1% carb. chrome plated	Acetyl Copolymer	2100

Supporting Maths

$$SIN = \frac{Opposite}{Hypotenuse}$$

$$COS = \frac{Adjacent}{Hypotenuse}$$

$$TAN = \frac{Opposite}{Adjacent}$$

$$Hypotenuse^2 = Side\ 1^2 + Side\ 2^2$$

$$Wheel\ Frequency\ (CPM) = 187.8 \sqrt{\frac{Wheel\ Rate\ (in/lbs)}{Sprung\ Wt\ (lbs)}}$$

$$Coil\ rate\ (ins/lbs) = Crush\ (ins) \times load\ (lbs)$$

$$Coil\ fitted\ rate\ (ins/lbs) = \frac{Coil\ rate\ (ins/lbs)}{Suspension\ leverage}$$

$$Wheel\ rate\ (ins/lbs) = \frac{Coil\ rate\ (ins/lbs)}{Suspension\ leverage^2}$$

$$Angular\ Rate\ (rollbar) = \frac{19700 \times OD^4}{Bar\ length}$$

$$AR\ (tube)\ (in/lbs/degree) = \frac{19700 \times (OD^4 - ID^4)}{Tube\ length}$$

$$Linear\ Rate\ (rollbar\ or\ tube)\ (in/lbs) = \frac{Angular\ Rate}{Lever\ Arm\ \times \frac{\pi}{180}}$$

$$Lever\ Arm\ Ratio = \frac{Bar\ pickup\ movement\ (ins)}{Wheel\ movement\ (ins)}$$

$$Bar\ Roll\ Resistance\ (in/lbs/degree) = \frac{Bar\ linear\ rate \times (Wheel\ movement \times Bar\ PU)^2 \times Track^2 \times \pi}{180}$$

$$Spring\ Roll\ Resistance\ (in/lbs/degree) = \frac{Spring\ rate \times Track^2 \times \pi}{(Wheel\ movement \div Spring\ movement)^2 \times 2 \times 180}$$

Springs in parallel   Combined rate = Rate coil A + Rate coil B

$$Spring\ in\ series\quad Combined\ rate = \frac{Rate\ coil\ A \times Rate\ coil\ B}{Rate\ coil\ A + Rate\ coil\ B}$$

Effect of antiroll bar
on single wheel bump.

$$Rate\ of\ spring\ in\ bump = Rate\ of\ coil\ A + \frac{Rate\ coil\ A \times Bar\ rate}{Rate\ coil\ A + Bar\ rate}$$

Glossary

A-arm See wishbone.

Acceleration What happens to a human being or other object in bump (vertical) cornering (lateral) and in braking/accelerating (longitudinal).

Accelerometer Device which measures acceleration.

Ackerman (angle) Method devised by gentleman of the same name which turns the inner front wheel into a tighter circle than the outer to minimise or eliminate scrub in a corner.

Active suspension "Live" or "thinking" pre-programmable, on-board computer control of suspension to retain virtues while eliminating undesirable aspects. Much easier said than done.

Actuator Hydraulic ram that translates pressure into movement (displacement).

Amplifier Not Hi-Fi in our context - see servo.

Anti-dive (angle) Geometric method of reducing attempts by car to scrape its nose on the ground under braking by tilting inboard suspension pick-up points (see also Anti-squat).

Anti roll bar Length of tube or rod linked to the suspension in such a way that if a car wishes to roll in a corner it must twist the bar (see Blades).

Anti-squat As anti-dive, but applied to the rear of the vehicle to reduce or prevent "sitting down" under acceleration.

Axle weight Portion or percentage of the gross weight borne by the front or rear pair of tyres.

Ballistic recoil Opposite reaction to a mechanical load input.

Beam axle Early method (not to mention commercial vehicles in the Eighties) of mounting the front wheels at each end of a solid steel bar.

Blades Flat, tapered steel arms on one or both ends of anti-roll bars. Rotation flat to edge-on increases, and the reverse decreases the roll resistance of the bar in a complex fashion.

Bump (Also jounce, heave, bounce) Total upward movement of wheel from static ride height (see also Droop).

Bump steer Front wheels altering their direction without the driver moving the steering wheel. Can also occur with certain linkages on rear suspension, when it feels very peculiar.

Camber Wheel angle seen from head-on. "Bow legged" (or tops wider apart than bottoms) is positive, "knock kneed" is negative. Positive in road cars but normally nil - 2.5 degrees negative in race cars.

Caster "Lean back" angle of top pivot behind bottom pivot of a front upright seen from the side of the car. Ranges from zero to eight or more degrees. Less you can get away with the better as extreme caster gives heavy steering.

Canard Small wing mounted low down at front of car.

Centre of Gravity Point at which the whole vehicle would always stay perfectly balanced whether on its side, nose, or even upside down. Difficult to locate precisely but close estimates are practical.

Channel Route along which a single set of electronic signals travels back and forth.

Chapman strut Chapman's adaptation of the MacPherson strut to use on the rear of the original Elite. The coil spring and damper are mounted integrally and above the hub, which has bottom locating links to the chassis.

Chip Nothing to do with fish. Slang; see

Integrated Circuit.

Closed loop Sometimes called "feedback loop": a circuit that allows an actuator's own actions to trigger what it will do next.

Coil See Spring.

Compound See Tyres.

Contact patch Area of a tyre that actually touches the road. Surprisingly small.

Corner weight Portion of a car's total weight on any particular tyre contact patch. Fronts should match each other, as should rears.

Damper (Shock, shocker, shock absorber) Device to control the natural oscillation of a spring. Usually a piston forcing oil through carefully designed valves. Sometimes combined with remote air reservoir. Valving can be fixed or widely adjustable.

Digital process(ing) Translating signals from the suspension's movement into computer language.

de Dion axle (or tube) Rear axle design devised by the French count of that name (or possibly by one of his mechanics, M. Bouton) in which the differential is chassis mounted with drive shafts out to the hubs which are joined together by a solid but light tube.

Droop Total downward movement of a wheel from static ride height (see also Bump).

Flap Adjustable section mounted on the trailing edge of a wing to alter its effective angle of attack and thus its downforce.

Gross weight Total weight of vehicle. Regulations may define this as "dry" without fuel or even water and oil, and without driver. For real life calculations, add them all in.

Gurney flap Small vertical flange on a wing or flap trailing edge producing a vortex to help air below the wing keep its flow pattern - named after American driver Dan Gurney who (perhaps) did it first.

Hardware Boxes, wires, screens, etc., that make up the physical equipment in a computer installation.

Health monitoring Nothing to do with the driver's wellbeing. The computer switches on its own warning light if all is not well.

Heave One of four modes used in Lotus Active suspension control. When all four wheels move up or down at equal speed. Four wheels at a time version of bump and droop.

Instantaneous Roll Centre Another of those theoretical points in space, both invisible and moving; where lines projected from the suspension links intersect, and about which a wheel is considered to rotate when moving in bump and droop. See also Roll Centre and Swing Axle Length.

Integrated circuit A number of components forming a circuit in one package, usually silicon and miniaturised. A collection of such circuits becomes a "chip".

Interface Trendy word for a joint or connection between two pieces of compatable electrical equipment. Very often two matching plugs.

Intermediate See tyres.

Jacking Effect of certain suspension geometries with high roll centres (notably swing axles) which cause a car to lift as it attempts to rotate around the outer tyre contact patch and eventually roll over.

King Pin Inclination Angle between vertical and a line connecting top and bottom pivots of a front suspension upright seen from head on.

Leaf See Spring.

Loop gains Amplifying a tiny signal into a bigger one in a loop circuit.

Microcomputer Very small computer. Followed mini-computer into use as computers shrank from room size to large desk to small box and less.

Microprocessor Chip inside a computer which controls its activities and the instructions it sends out.

Modal In particular, the Lotus approach to suspension analysis and control by breaking all movements down into four basic modes (see also Heave, Pitch, Roll and Warp).

Monostable Electronic equivalent of a headlight flasher switch: always in condition "A" but can be ordered temporarily to "B".

Panhard rod After the Frenchman of Panhard and Levassor (very early car builders) fame. A transversely mounted rod, from chassis on one side to solid axle on the other to prevent sideways movement.

Pitch Rotation of a vehicle about its transverse axis in nosedive or squat.

Programme Set of instructions which tell a computer what to do in any particular situation.

Pull rod Link from top of an upright to bottom of a spring suspension unit (usually through a pivot bar or bellcrank of some type).

Push rod Same as pull rod, except working upwards under compression from the bottom of an upright to a spring suspension unit.

Roll Rotation or lean of a vehicle under cornering forces.

Roll Axis Longitudinal line around which a vehicle rolls (joins front and rear roll centres).

Roll Centre Invisible moving point about which a vehicle is considered to rotate in a corner. Easy to plot in static situation, but far from easy once the vehicle is moving.

Roll Moment Leverage exerted by a car attempting to roll.

Roll Stiffness Resistance to roll of a vehicle when cornering, exerted mainly by the anti-roll bars and to a lesser degree by the suspension springs.

Rack and Pinion Steering mechanism - toothed bar pushed from side to side when a small cog connected to the steering wheel is rotated. Universal in sports and racing cars.

Rake (angle) When a vehicle is set other than parallel to the ground. Normally nose-down to some degree for aerodynamic reasons.

Ride Height Static clearance of a vehicle above the ground which controls the vertical height in space of the inboard suspension pick-up points, as well as all bodywork heights that might be specified by the regulations.

Rocking arm A stressed top wishbone working like a see-saw with the wheel at one end and a coil/damper unit at the other.

Scoop Nose rise under braking. A phenomena available with Active suspension, but not in popular use.

Self-centre Tendency of the front wheels to return to the straight- ahead position during and after a turn, caused geometrically by the caster angle.

Sensor Device which translates a physical happening (eg. movement, speed, temperature rise or fall) into an electrical signal.

Servo amplifier Boosts the signals to/from a servo valve.

Servo valve High speed hydraulic switching valves which change push into pull and vice-versa within an actuator.

Shock absorber See Damper.

Slick See Tyre.

Software Collection of instructions for a computer stored in various ways including on magnetic disc and tape.

Solid axle Alternative name for beam axle but more generally a steel rear axle case containing crown wheel, pinion, differential, bearings, etc., and carrying the brakes, drums and drive shafts.

Splitter Thin horizontal ledge, often adjustable for width, on front bottom edge of bodywork designed to persuade as much air as possible over the top of the vehicle rather than underneath it.

Spoiler Usually a lip or ridge on the bodywork designed to enhance, alter or destroy smooth airflow at a particular point.

Spring Coil, leaf, torsion bar, rubber block, etc., which provides the squashable cushion in a suspension.

Spring rate Load necessary to deflect any spring by a given distance (usually lbs./in. or Newtons/mm.).

Sprung weight See weight.

Steering arm Lever on the front upright through which the steering forces are exerted (usually a forged finger or a pair of bolt-on alloy plates) attached to the track rod end.

Swing Axle Suspension design in which the wheel mounts on a single solid link attached near to, on, or beyond the centre line of the vehicle.

Swing Axle Length Distance between the Instantaneous Roll Centre and the wheel. Varies continually during suspension movement.

Synthetic spring Word for what an actuator becomes when working.

Toe-in When a pair of wheels seen in plan view are not parallel but are closer at the front than at the rear.

Toe-out Reverse of toe-in.

Toe control link Strut between chassis and rear upright (usually threaded left/right each end for rapid adjustment) giving control of rear toe.

Top hat Bush with bigger diameter flange at one end.

Torque tube A tubular extension bolted to the front of a solid axle differential housing, which locates it fore and aft, and also deals with braking and acceleration twisting loads.

Track Distance between the centre lines of

a pair of tyres (front or rear).

Track rod Bar connecting a rack and pinion to the steering arm.

Track rod end Spherical joint at the outboard end of a track rod.

Transducer Device which translates movement into electrical signals.

Transient manoeuvre The move from one state or condition to another, usually by a steering movement - the perfect vehicle example is taking an "S" bend.

Tyre Round, black and one on each corner. But also - compounds; specific rubber mix on the working face - slicks; completely smooth surfaced with only wear check slots - intermediates; light/medium cut tread for damp/dusty surfaces - wets; complex and deep pattern designed to clear substantial water from beneath the tyre - control; type, pattern or make designated in the rules as the only type to be used - cross ply; carcase in which the fabric layers run from side to side but at varying angles - radials; carcase in which the main load bearing layer (often of steel wire rather than fabric or synthetic weave) runs completely round the tyre beneath the tread compound.

Upright Casting or fabrication which carries the hub, bearings, oil seals and often single or twin brake calipers for independent suspension.

Warp Mode of Lotus Active when the front and rear axles roll opposite ways and amounts.

Watt's linkage All too often written without the apostrophe, but James Watt invented it for his steam engines. Automotively it is usually employed to locate a solid rear axle transversely with great accuracy while still permitting it to rise, fall or tilt freely.

Weight Sprung; parts of a vehicle supported by the springs. Generally taken as gross weight, less unsprung weight. Unsprung; normally taken as wheels, tyres, hubs, outboard brakes, etc., plus half the weight of any linkages, outboard coils, dampers, etc.

Wet See tyres.

Wheel frequency Rhythmic speed at which a wheel/hub/upright will bounce up and down if not damped. In CPM (cycles per minute) or Hz (Hertz, or cycles per second). Low is soft, high is hard in suspension terms.

Wheelbase Distance between front and rear wheel hub lines.

Wheel rate Spring rate as seen by the wheel after suspension leverage effects.

Wing Precisely what you see on an aircraft but upside down so that it will press down rather than lift when moving through the air.

Wishbone Roughly vee-shaped link joining an upright to the car. Deceptively simple in appearance but with much know-how in its material, stressing and manufacture.

Yaw Rotation of a vehicle about its vertical axis - "hanging the tail out" in most people's terms but also sideways lurch in strong crosswinds.

Index